To the Memory of My Mother,

Richelene Whitaker Mitchell

(1934 — 1975)

For she is wise, if I can judge of her,
And fair she is, if that mine eyes be true,
And true she is, as she hath prov'd herself;
And therefore, like herself, wise, fair, and true,
Shall she be placed in my constant soul.

- The Merchant of Venice, II. vi

Scattered Pictures
Reflections of an American Muslim

An anthology of essays by

Imām Zaid Shākir

ZAYTUNA INSTITUTE

Published by Zaytuna Institute
Printed in the United States of America

ISBN: 0-9792281-1-5

Zaytuna Institute
631 Jackson Street
Hayward, California 94544
info@zaytuna.org
www.zaytuna.org

Contents

Transliteration Key

ﷺ – Invocation of “peace and blessings of God be upon him” that follows references to the Prophet Muhammad ﷺ

عليه السلام – Invocation of “peace be upon him” that follows references to other recognized Prophets

Ā – A doubling in length (holding for two counts) of the “a”

Ī – A doubling in length (holding for two counts) of the “i”

Ū – A doubling in length (holding for two counts) of the “u”

Ḍ – An emphatic “th,” as in the word *th*is

Ḥ – An emphatic “h” or “kh,” while constricting the middle of the throat

Ṣ – An emphatic “s,” with the tongue behind the upper teeth

Ṭ – An emphatic “t”, with the tongue behind the upper teeth

Ẓ – An emphatic “th”, with the tongue behind the upper teeth

’ – A distinctive glottal stop made deep in the throat that is often used at the end of a word to indicate an abrupt stop, and also to concatenate two words

ᶜ – A distinctive Semitic sound that sounds like a vowel

About the Author

Imām Zaid Shākir was born in Berkeley, California and accepted Islām in 1977 while serving in the United States Air Force. He earned a BA with honors in International Relations at the American University in Washington, D.C. and an MA in Political Science from Rutgers University. While overseas in Egypt, Syria, and Morocco, he studied Arabic and traditional Islāmic sciences including Islāmic law, Qur'ān, and Islāmic spirituality. He co-founded Masjid al-Islām in Connecticut and taught Political Science at Southern Connecticut State University. He has translated several books from Arabic into English including *The Heirs of the Prophets.* Imām Zaid Shākir currently teaches full-time at the Zaytuna Institute in Hayward, California as a scholar-in-residence.

Acknowledgements

The people who have helped in bringing this project to fruition are many. Were I to endeavor to mention them all by name, I would do a grave injustice to those whose contributions were important but whose names I may inadvertently omit. To avoid doing so, I will I express my general gratitude to all of my teachers, Muslim and non-Muslim, who have contributed to my spiritual and intellectual development. I also express my deepest appreciation to my colleagues who have read versions of the articles and essays gathered here and have offered valuable and necessary suggestions. May God have mercy on them.

I would also like to thank my students. My interaction with them provided a forum for me to explore many of the ideas that found their way into this work. Their energy and insightful feedback are an indispensable component of the book. May God preserve them all.

I must express my indebtedness to the staff, volunteers, and supporters of the Zaytuna Institute. They have provided the tangible and intangible support that allowed the idea of this work to manifest itself in the finished form before you. Special thanks go to those who have worked on proofreading, layout, cover design, and all of the other technical aspects of the work. May God reward them abundantly.

I would be remiss if I did not thank my wife, whose hard work behind the scenes is an integral part of anything I may do or accomplish in the public sphere. May God bless her.

Finally, I would like to express my deep appreciation for my immediate family. They have provided the culture of love and nurturing that helped to lay the foundation of my life. May God guide them all.

Publishing Credits

Preliminary versions of some of the material contained in this work appeared in *Seasons Journal* ("Flight From the Masjid," Spring/Summer 2003; "Jihād is Not Perpetual Warfare," Autumn/Winter 2003-2004; "Islām and the Nationalist Question," Spring/Summer 2004; "Islam, The Prophet Muḥammad, and Blackness," Spring/Summer 2005); *Cross Currents* ("American Muslims and a Meaningful Human Rights Discourse," Winter 2003); *American Journal of Islamic Social Sciences* ("Reflections on the Tsunami," Winter 2005); *Zaytuna Institute Website.* <http://www.zaytuna.org> (2005, "We Are All Collateral Damage," "Abraham's Story," "Reflections on Black History Month," "Trees," and "Peace and Justice in Islām).

Foreword

Ours are difficult, confusing, and in many ways contradictory times. Technological advances are so profound that many observers feel we are entering a new axial age. Future institutions, new ways of thinking, and new ways of living are being fashioned in these times. However, despite the profundity of the advances characterizing our lives, the reemergence of many of our old prejudices, biases, and hatreds threatens to undo many of the great human achievements of the past century. The great expansion of trade, which led to a near universal rise in living standards, is breaking down into a world where the gap between the haves and have-nots, both within individual states and internationally, has never been greater. The regime of international law and organization that facilitated an international order where major conflagrations between interstate actors were becoming anomalous, is threatening to degenerate into a state where warfare again becomes the accepted norm to resolve disputes between contending groups.

Perhaps the reemergence of old, destructive ways of thinking is no more visible than in the rise of mutually-excluding, narrow religious fundamentalisms. Religious passions are being stoked across the globe, and in the ensuing blaze, it becomes extremely difficult for advocates of the common good to be heard, and understanding inevitably wanes. Deep and damaging polarization may result if current trends are not challenged. This situation has motivated this writer to try to contribute what is intended to be a voice of reason and understanding in ongoing discussions whose outcomes will go a long way towards determining the future of our planet.

The issues dealt with in this book are approached from an Islāmic analytical framework. It has been one of the goals of the Zaytuna Institute, with which I am proudly affiliated, to use the deep reservoir of traditional Islāmic knowledge to provide insight into and solutions for our contemporary condition. By traditional Islāmic knowledge, I refer not only to the Qur'ān and the prophetic tradition (*Sunna*), but also to the wealth of jurisprudential and exegetical writings that have helped to insure the historic integrity and continuity of the Islāmic project. I also refer to the methodological tools that have allowed for a flexible, practical, and dynamic application of Islāmic law. Only by immersing ourselves in that reservoir will Muslims be capable of making an intelligible contribution towards addressing the challenging issues of our times.

However, that knowledge is not applicable in a vacuum. It must be applied in the context in which we find ourselves: the context of advanced western civilization. That being the case, we must have knowledge of this civilization and its intellectual tradition. Only then can traditional Islāmic knowledge be relevant and make an effective contribution to the ongoing advance of human civilization. It is from these twin traditions, one rooted in the East, the other in the West, that these reflections emerge.

I begin with a brief biographical sketch, *The Making of a Muslim*. Who is the writer holding the pen, and what are the developments that have molded him? Many times, when we find something of great interest in our readings, we are moved to ask these questions. I have endeavored to provide an answer by describing the factors that led this American Muslim to hold a very anti-American attitude—I might even say a bitter contempt for the land of my birth—followed by an examination of some of factors that led to a moderation of that position.

We Are All Collateral Damage, written in the immediate aftermath of the London subway bombings, illustrates the fact that innocents on both "sides" of the terror war are reduced to collateral damage by the maniacal violence perpetrated by the actors of a cruel farce. Although I do not elaborate on the many reasons I view this "war" as a farce, I do emphasize that until all sides respect the sanctity of civilian life, there will be little progress towards a meaningful resolution of the deepening crisis between the West and the Muslim world.

Abraham's Story عليه السلام emphasizes the importance of being "large" people who are willing to follow the example of Abraham عليه السلام, both in his sterling character and his intrepid leadership traits. Developing such character will require a new generation of Muslim scholars who are not only versed in the rich Islāmic intellectual tradition, but are also cognizant of contemporary issues, trends, and intellectual currents. Such a cadre of intellectuals will have to avoid the conservatism that has rendered many traditional Islāmic scholars ineffective here in the West and the isolating elitism that tends to characterize those Islāmic scholars whose primary training has taken place in the confines of the Western academy.

I then turn to an examination of the concept of nationalism, attempting to develop an Islāmic critique of what is often a destructive idea. That critique, entitled *Islām and the Question of Nationalism*, revolves around the universality of the Islāmic message and the unity of humanity posited by Islām. I also examine some of the critical concepts that underlie nationalist thinking and examine how fear, anger, and victimization are manipulated to foster a mentality open to the appeals of nationalist demigods. This article concludes with some suggestions of how Islām can foster a social psychology conducive to a more inclusive view of humanity and society.

The following essay examines the attitude of the Prophet Muḥammad ﷺ towards blackness. *Islām, the Prophet Muḥammad ﷺ, and Blackness* opens with an examination of some of the significations associated with blackness in both the Arabic and English languages along with a look at the positive signification associated with the concept of blackness in the Qur'ān and Arabic lexical sources. The article concludes with a detailed examination of some of the ways the Prophet Muḥammad ﷺ attempted to rid his society of the negative color consciousness that still afflicts many Muslim societies.

Reflections on Black History Month concentrates on the importance of American Muslims identifying with African American history. As recent research has revealed, a significant percentage of the African people brought to this country during the slavery epoch were Muslims. Hence, their story in this land is part of the greater Islāmic narrative. Sincerely identifying with that history affords a great deal of legitimacy and authenticity to the Muslims who have migrated here from other lands. I also address how important it is for Muslims, especially African American Muslims, to address the issue of racism that still plagues our society. However, to effectively address that issue, all efforts must be used to avoid the delusion-generating triumvirate of rage, victimization, and vengeance. ne of the greatest manifestations of the delusional thinking that may ensue if those sentiments are given sway is the tendency to see the situation as mirroring that of colonized majorities in the "Third World" and then viewing liberationist strategies that have failed there, availing us here.

Not Muslim Zionists is an article I wrote 13 years ago. However, its message is still relevant. This is especially true as Muslims in many places are wrestling with the issue of balancing between the adherence to the ethical ideals of Islām and political expediency. The consequences of what can happen to a religion when political expediency wins out are poignantly illustrated by the intertwined histories of Judaism and Zionism. I warn that we as Muslims should not make the mistake of the Zionists by sacrificing our religious ethics on the altar of the national interest.

Trees is a brief essay written in the aftermath of the demise of the "Bowing Tree" that graced the grounds of the Zaytuna Institute until this past winter. A fixture on our property, its passing reminds us of our own mortality. This essay is rooted in Joyce Kilmer's reflection on trees and tries to capture the spirit of awe that can be inspired by reflecting deeply on that magnificent creation and, more importantly, by reflecting deeply on its creator.

After this interlude, in a critical essay entitled *Flight From the Mosque*, I attempt to examine some of the reasons why various categories of Muslims are either alienated from or not attracted to the mosque. The essay opens by examining the definition of the word *masjid* (the Arabic equivalent of mosque), and then attempts to briefly look at some of the reasons many people are being alienated from an institution that has historically been an open refuge for the entire community of believers. The article concludes with some practical measures that may serve to attract and keep a healthy, representative cross-section of Muslims in the mosques.

If the mosque is to be a healthy and vibrant institution, its educational role is critical, for the ignorance of Islām that exists among the general public is to a large extent a reflection of the religious ignorance rampant in the Muslim community. In this regard, we Muslims need to be reminded of the primacy of peace and justice in our religion as well as the nature of the relationship between these two terms. This is the topic of the next essay, *Peace and Justice in Islām*, which introduces the reader to the comprehensive nature of peace in Islām and the incumbency of pursuing justice. However, the nature of the justice pursued should follow from its signs and portents, which include generosity, humility, and mercy.

In today's political climate, perhaps no Islāmic issue is as misunderstood as jihād. Unfortunately, bigoted polemicists, pushing an agenda contrary to the best interests of this country, are attempting to equate jihād to the old communist or fascist threats. Claiming that jihād involves an obligation of permanent, unmitigated warfare against non-Muslim nations and peoples, they assert that this country will have to be eternally vigilant, a vigilance that leads to massive defense spending and the right to preemptively attack any nation deemed to pose a threat to our national interests. In *Jihād Is Not Perpetual Warfare*, I endeavor to debunk the charge that jihād involves an unrelenting war against non-Muslims and thereby precludes Muslims from accepting the regime of international law that facilitates peace as a norm in international relations. My argument should not be construed, as some critics have attempted to imply, that jihād is nullified as a legal obligation. There are circumstances when a Muslim nation may be forced to take up arms. However, that obligation does not preclude, as I argue, Muslim individuals and nations peacefully coexisting with those who have expressed peaceful intentions and goodwill towards them.

Ultimate justice is for Almighty God. However, we oftentimes lose sight of that fact and tend to question His mercy and justice when disasters such as the recent Tsunami occur. In, *Reflections on the Tsunami*, I attempt to contextualize the Tsunami by placing it in an Islāmic analytical framework, focusing on the reality of the Hereafter and the otherworldly compensation promised the believer for any worldly suffering. I also attempt to remind the Muslim that none of us will ever suffer in the world the difficulties that were visited upon the Messenger of God, Muḥammad ﷺ. Calamities, such as the Tsunami also involve, in many instances, events that have been foretold by our Prophet ﷺ. That being the case, their occurrence should only strengthen our faith and inspire us to do more to alleviate the suffering of those afflicted.

American Muslims, Human Rights, and the Challenge of September 11 examines how the horrific events of that day force Muslims here in the West to move away from the clichés, slogans, and superficial analyses that have done little to help us address the very real issues confronting our community. Studies of the idea of human rights in both the Western and Islāmic traditions show that there is a human rights imperative at work in the Islāmic community as that community has been historically manifested in America. The tragedies of September 11 have provided a backdrop for many antagonistic elements to challenge the basis of any Islāmic human rights regime. In their minds, Islām is viewed as a barbaric atavism incapable of contributing in a meaningful way to the modern social project. There is a challenge implicit in their words, and it forces us as Muslims to deepen and refine our understanding of the idea of human rights.

In the final article of this compilation, I add my voice to the discussion that arose as a result of the "historic" female-led Friday prayer. *The Issue of Female Prayer Leadership* looks at the issue from the linguistic and jurisprudential sources of Sunnī Islām, the literature dealing with the classification of prophetic tradition, lexicography, and the writings of leading orientalists. If nothing else, it should reveal to the reader the richness of both the Islāmic intellectual heritage and the depth of traditional legal thought. For Muslims, it is hoped that this examination will also engender a healthier respect for the scholars of this tradition and encourage more deliberation and deliberateness before speaking, oftentimes flippantly, on very serious and consequential issues.

Finally, I wish to mention a few matters associated with my treatment of Arabic passages, phrases, and words. All of the translations of Qur'ānic verses and prophetic traditions are my own. The

Qur'ānic passages have been italicized in the text and are followed by the chapter and verse numbers placed between brackets. Brief prophetic traditions are mentioned between quotation marks in the main body of the text, while lengthier passages are indented. I have chosen to include the diacritical marks commonly used when transliterating Arabic words to assist those who are interested in proper pronunciation. A transliteration key is provided on page vi. I have also retained the Arabic feature that distinguishes between "sun" and "moon" letters, after the definite article "al," as in "ash-Shams," and "al-Qamar." Because many readers may not have exposure to and subsequent knowledge of commonly-used Arabic words and terminology within the framework of Islām, I have endeavored to translate the meanings of individual Arabic words used in the text and then present the transliterated form of the word immediately thereafter in parentheses.

Hopefully, this brief introduction has motivated you to forge on. It is my hope that your understanding of what Islām says regarding the issues examined here will be deepened. More importantly, it is hoped that your understanding about what Islām might say on many other related issues will similarly be enhanced. If that is the case, I praise God, for all good and benefit arises from His boundless grace. On the other hand, if you come away from this engagement confused or unfulfilled, that is owing to my own shortcomings. I have done my best, dealing with a number of limitations, to make a humble contribution to the ever-expanding literature on Islām in America and more importantly, I think, to the ever-expanding literature by Muslims in America.

Imām Zaid Shākir
July 2005

The Making of a Muslim

I was born in Berkeley, California, May 24, 1956, the second of seven siblings. At the time, my father was in the U.S. Navy, stationed on the West Coast. After moving with his fledging family to San Diego, he left the military and returned to his birthplace of Battle Creek, Michigan. My father was born in 1932, one of five children. His great grandfather was Irish, the source of our family name, Mitchell.

My mother, born in Hamilton, Georgia, was one of thirteen children. Their father was an African American sharecropper. My mother was a brilliant student. She is reputed to have never received anything other than an "A" grade for every class she ever took at any level of school. Sensing her brilliance, her parents sent her to Philadelphia for high school. During that time she stayed with the family of an older brother who had migrated north. Upon graduating from high school, before entering college, she journeyed to Battle Creek to live with her older sister, Gertrude. It was during that time that she met my father. She would never attend college, as they were married soon thereafter and started their family. Looking for an opportunity to improve his chances of raising a stable family, my father joined the Navy, which led to our family residing in California at the time of my birth and that of my older sister and two younger brothers.

After his discharge from the Navy, he left California. Upon returning home, my father, an accomplished saxophone player, began to intensify his pursuit of a career in music. This led to instability in the family, which culminated in my mother returning with us children to Georgia so she could be close to her family. After spending a year with my older sister on our grandparents' farm while my mother got situated in Atlanta, we settled in Carver Homes, a large public housing project in South West Atlanta. Life in those projects provided the experiences that form some of the most distant memories I have of my childhood.

Those memories are couched in black. All of the residents of the projects were African Americans, we attended an all-black elementary school, and all of our teachers and instructors were African Americans. When we would go to the family farm in Hamilton to harvest cotton—I actually remember dragging the long sack behind me and stuffing it with cotton—we were surrounded by black folks. The only time I can remember even seeing any white people was while accompanying my mother on a periodical shopping expedition to downtown Atlanta.

Near the end of my third year in elementary school, I learned that my mother and father had reconciled and that he had left the music business and gotten a steady job at a Sears store in West Hartford, Connecticut. We packed our bags, placed everything that would fit into our station wagon and the U-Haul trailer it had in tow, and headed north. Any personal or household items that would not fit into those two conveyances were left piled up on the curb in front of our apartment.

Arriving in Connecticut, we moved into another large housing project, Pinnacle Heights, in New Britain, then dubbed the "Hardware Capital of the World." When we arrived, the projects were still predominantly white. However, that situation did not last too long. In a few short years, the Irish "Smiths" next door were to be replaced by the African American "Johnsons." The Italian "Mirantes" two doors down were to be replaced by the African American "Daniels." On the other side of our unit, the Jewish "Prices" were to be replaced by another African American family. Other white families were replaced by the "Mecados", "Maldanados", and other Latino families. By the time I entered high school, Pinnacle Heights was an overwhelmingly African American and Puerto Rican bastion with only a few white families—families too poor to move elsewhere.

Unfortunately, my parents' reconciliation was short-lived. We were soon alone with my mother, far away from her home, scraping to get by, but happy nonetheless. My mother's intellect was not stifled by the fact that she was now a welfare mother, struggling single-handedly to raise a family that had expanded to seven children. She was an avid reader and a controversial writer. Her editorials and articles appeared frequently in the *New Britain Herald* and the *Hartford Courant*. Her poignant views on issues relating to race and social justice earned her the wrath of various white supremacy groups who would frequently send threatening hate mail to our home. Such hatred, among other things, led my mother, who was not a racist, to view Idi Amīn as a hero for his expulsion of Europeans from Uganda. I remember reading some of those letters and reflecting on their message of hate. A little later in life they would help to fuel my anti-Americanism.

I experienced many things during my high school years that would add to my growing bitterness. Some were small, such as the callousness of our football coach who would come to the projects diligently every morning to give me and a group of my friends, who also played on the team, a ride to school, sparing us the inconvenience of waiting for the bus. However, as soon as the last game of our senior year was over, he did not know us. He would pass us in the hallway of school and not even spare a glance in our direction. This callous exploitation was not lost on me. I had literally given this man an arm, a severely separated shoulder my senior year, and a leg, which I broke my freshman year. Now I could not even get him to say hello!

Other events were more significant. Among them were the murders of two unarmed teenagers by two white New Britain police officers. One victim was a young Puerto Rican named Miguel Arroyo; the second, a troubled young African American teen, my younger brother's friend, Papo Post. In the aftermath of these shootings, there were no inquiries, no suspensions, no nothing. Two young lives were senselessly terminated, and it was business as usual in the city.

The event that was probably most influential in inspiring me to seriously search for a way to help reform others occurred during my first year at Central Connecticut State University. I had been accepted to CCSU as part of a minority equal opportunity program. In high school I was addicted to sports. I played football and ran track. I was constantly training, running, lifting weights with no smoking, drinking, or drug use. I ate healthily before it became popular to do so. However, the shoulder injury terminated my football career, and as a result there were some changes in my lifestyle.

One night as I was walking home after a party in the Mount Pleasant housing projects, which we used to call "Sparkle City" because it was littered with so much broken glass, a young Puerto Rican girl—she could not have been more than ten years old—ran out into the bitterly cold winter night screaming, "Why doesn't anyone love me? Why doesn't anyone love me?" Her cry echoed in my head and penetrated into my heart. I thought about the difficulties so many people were having in these seemingly God-forsaken places. The drugs, alcoholism, teen pregnancies, violence, and broken homes had wreaked havoc on so many innocent lives. Right then I made up my mind to work for a change.

The first place I began looking for that change was in my religion; surely God would provide the guidance that would lead to a better way. When I started that quest, I did not know a thing about Christian theology or the history of the religion despite being born into a Baptist family. I could not begin to explain, even at the simplest level, the difference between a Baptist and a Catholic, or between a Presbyterian and an Episcopalian. I was clueless. As I discovered the numerous, glaring contradictions in the Bible, along with the history of the resolution of the struggle between the Unitarians and their opponents, I concluded that the entire religion was man-made. I consciously rejected it and became an atheist.

In January of 1975, I met a political activist at CCSU who introduced me to the literature of the black liberation struggle. Beginning with George Jackson's *Soledad Brother*, I avidly read a wide array of increasingly radical leftist writings. I came to despise Christianity, seeing it as the ideological wing of a European expansionist imperialist agenda. "Take our bibles and give us your land and resources." During this period, I would not set foot into a church. Having obtained a car at the age of 18, a 1965 Oldsmobile Dynamic 88, the first car anyone in our family owned since my father left over ten years earlier, I would drive my mother to church and wait in the parking lot for the service to end to bring her home.

Two things were to arrest my deeper involvement in the black liberation movement. The first was my rediscovery of God. That happened suddenly and strangely. One day—I don't recall the exact circumstances—I happened upon one of those small rectangular Christian comic books. The author was not arguing for the truth of Christian doctrine, rather he was arguing for the existence of God. His argument was basically the argument of causation, that it was impossible to create something from nothing, no matter how hard intelligent minds tried. Hence, to assume that this creation began from nothing is to assume the impossible. There had to be a creator who created something from the nothing. For me the only other alternative, that matter always existed, was untenable. Secondly, he argued that to assume that a simple inorganic substance, once created, could in isolation take on the properties of life, gaining the ability to grow and reproduce, without a life-giver, also involved the impossible. Finally, were we to assume for the sake of argument that our primal substance spontaneously came to life, it is impossible to conceive of it accidentally evolving into the vast, complex, dynamic universe that surrounds us. Hence, he argued, there has to be a creator, a life-giver, and an evolver. I would later learn that these were all understood as names or attributes of God in Islāmic theology.

At that time, I reflected deeply on the author's arguments. I tried to reconcile them with the atheistic communist philosophy predicated on historical and dialectical materialism. I would always be led back to a question, "In the dialectical argument, where did the first thesis come from?" My failure to get an adequate answer from any of my comrades, led to my soon abandoning both communism and atheism. Indeed, as I saw it, there had to be a creator.

The second event was the sudden passing of my mother. In the spring of 1975, she suffered an aneurysm and passed away at New Britain General Hospital after spending a few days in a coma. Her death was tragic and ironic. During the entire time we had lived in Connecticut, we had the same increasingly shabby furniture. Just as there was no extra money to buy a car, there was no money to buy new furniture. What we did have reflected the wear and tear inflicted over the years by seven children of various ages. My mother scrimped and scraped to put aside enough money to buy a new living room set. The very afternoon that the new furniture was delivered and in place, and she got to see it, she suffered the aneurysm. I returned home in the evening from my part-time job to find that she had been rushed to the hospital.

It is hard for many Muslims, who are by and large a privileged class in this country, to conceive of the lives lived by the poor. I'll share a quote from my mother's unpublished journal to provide a glimpse at how the underclass lives,

> I'm sick, sick, and sick of this dreary dead-end existence. Sick, sick, sick of being stuck here in this junk filled house with no outlet, no money, no nothing. Sewing machine out of order; TV out of order; refrigerator out of order; stove just making it; winter coming with its necessities; and no money in sight to repair or replace or buy anything. I'm sick to my soul of scraping, squeezing and scrounging...[1]

Her tragic death catalyzed my desire to know God. I was on the path to Islām. However, at the moment I was alone and I had to survive. I managed to finish the semester at school. However, my life was starting to slowly unravel. I had three part-time jobs early that summer and ended up losing them all. The job I had during the school year in a Hallmark card shop downtown, I inexplicably left. I just stopped going to work and really placed the store owner in a bind, as I was a good worker and he had come to depend on me. I lost the other two jobs when I went to Washington D.C. for a rally to help free Joan Little and the Wilmington Ten. After that rally I went to Atlanta to visit my relatives. When I returned to Connecticut I was almost arrested, as one of my jobs was as a security guard and I had left with a set of the company's keys!

The next semester, I dropped out of college. I walked into the minority student affairs office and announced that I was leaving school. There was no effort made to talk me out of leaving, it was simply goodbye. I eventually ended up going to stay with my father in Michigan. I had despised him for most of my adolescence. The broken promises of Christmas and birthday gifts that never arrived, the foul treatment of my mother, and other real and imaginary issues combined to push me away from him. However, I was now desperate and needed a roof over my head. My stay with him was short-lived. I was too bitter to be compassionate and understanding towards his plight or his side of the story. Only Islāmic teachings on the rights and duties to one's parents would eventually open my heart to him. However, I still needed a roof over my head and food in my stomach, and I wanted to continue my education. I found a way to do all of these things. I would join the armed forces.

I returned to Connecticut and promptly went to see a recruiter. This move was really depressing as I had been influenced by the communist doctrines I had studied and viewed the armed forces as epitomizing American imperialism. However, I reasoned that the Việt Nam war was over and I would not be called on to participate in killing anyone in the name of "God and country." I was forced to spend a few weeks in our old apartment, which had by now been taken over by my oldest sister and her own growing family. My youngest brother and sister were living with her along with her three young children. My second oldest sister, by now a sixteen year old mother, had moved out into an apartment of her own, and my other two brothers were in Michigan. I was soon in San Antonio, Texas, at Lackland Air Force Base, going through basic training.

After basic training I went to Denver, Colorado for technical school. As the school was finishing a previous session, I had a lot of spare time and resumed my spiritual quest. I ended up on the "mucusless diet," among other things, and would eventually, upon arriving at my permanent station at Barksdale Air Force Base, become involved with transcendental meditation. As my involvement with meditation deepened and my reading texts related to eastern mysticism progressed, I was feeling increasingly unfulfilled. I wanted to know God, but I found myself on a path that was leading to an enhanced knowledge of self. Perhaps this was God's way of introducing Himself to me. It is said that he who knows himself will know God. In any case, I gradually became disillusioned with eastern mysticism. I had been attracted to religion looking for a means to make things better for the people. I found the eastern approach to be very selfish. It was everything for me, but nothing for the people.

It was at this point that a close friend gave me a book on Islām, *Islām in Focus*, by the Egyptian writer Hamoudah ʿAbdul ʿĀṭī. When I read that book all of the questions I had concerning religion were answered. Who is God? What does He want from His servants? How do we follow in the footsteps of the Prophets as we go through our day? How do we begin to reform our society? In Islām, as it was presented in the pages of that book, I found all of my answers. I would soon publicly declare my conversion, in the spring of 1977 at a mosque affiliated with Imām Warith Deen Muḥammad, the successor of his father, Elijah Muḥammad, the deceased leader of what had been the Nation of Islām (NOI).

I was familiar with the NOI from New Britain. The group had a thriving branch in Hartford. Some of my friends had joined, and my mother had visited their temple. Many of the brothers used to come through our neighborhood selling fish and newspapers, both of which my mother would periodically buy. My mother was attracted by the group's discipline and the reforming power of their message. However, she saw beyond the false promise contained in its Black Nationalist agenda. She had come to understand that true human liberation would only come through the discovery of our true humanity. In her penetrating words, she describes that reality while commenting on the death of one of the youth in our neighborhood, an NOI member. She writes,

> But, Dear Self, I must talk softly and sadly with you for a while. Today at one o'clock an 18 year-old black youth that I knew will be buried. Self, it's so sad...so sad...he seemed like such a promising young man. And now he's gone, forever. Just when life should be beginning for him—it ended. He had some problems in school and in the community in his early teens. Then he started going to the Muslim temple. A great change for the better came over him.

> He sold the Muslim paper, *Muḥammad Speaks*, quietly and politely, often leaving us a free copy when I didn't have a quarter. And he went back to school and graduated this year. Then he got a job.
>
> The last time I saw him, he had come to our house to give Donna, Steve and I a ride to the temple. I wanted to go just to see what their meetings were like, to get a closer view of their philosophy—not to join. Self, admittedly I'm in sympathy to many of the concepts of their ideology, but I could never worship Muḥammad as my God.
>
> Anyway, that Sunday he came to pick us up. But Donna and Steve were still in bed, so I didn't go. I looked out the window as he walked back to his car. How nice and clean he looked in his burgundy knit dress jacket and checked flared trousers. How proudly he walked. He looked like a man—big, tall, and strong; and walked like a man—placing his footsteps firmly, as if he knew where he was going. In the Muslims he thought he had found the key to unlock the door to true black manhood. And maybe he had. Yet, maybe he hadn't. Maybe later in life he would have found that Elijah Muḥammad was not God's messenger and he had been misled. Maybe he would have found that he could not find his true manhood couched in an ideology but only in the deep recesses of himself and coming to grips with life as a human being—not as a Black Muslim. Nor even as a black man could he find his true place in life—only as a human being.
>
> But he had made a good beginning—from whatever source the seeds were sown. And I admired his struggle to grow into a man. Now he's gone—so suddenly. Choked to death on beans and rice... Rich people choke to death on steak; poor people choke to death on beans and rice, but they all go to the same place.[2]

Unfortunately, my mother never got an opportunity to hear more about Islām. She never got an opportunity to read *Islām in Focus*. I did, and I fully embraced the faith to the best of my ability. My family thought that embrace would be fleeting. However, weeks turned into months, months turned into years, years into decades, and by the grace of God, my faith has endured.

In 1979, the Iranian Islāmic Revolution occurred. I was stationed nearby in Turkey at the time, at Incirlik Airbase. I was barely affected by the revolution. I was too busy with my duties by day and propagating Islām by night. Along with my wife, we had formed a study group with other American Muslims stationed at Incirlik. We would organize programs about Islām for the other Americans on the base, until we were stopped by the Turkish base commander. He informed us that our activities were in violation of the laws of secular Turkey, which forbade the open propagation of religion. When we asked him why the laws didn't apply to all of the Christians who were openly organizing and propagating their religion on the base, he had no answer.

We gained converts. One of the most interesting stories is that of a young man from St. Louis, Missouri who converted to Islām after placing his face on the ground during the prayer, which he had joined out of boredom while waiting for a friend who had come to one of our classes. Returning to America, he proceeded to convert three of his brothers. Upon returning to the States myself, I ended up in Washington, D.C., where I would attend the American University. I also ended up being involved with an activist Islāmic organization, Jamāt al-Muslimeen. The Jamāt was very supportive of the Iranian Islāmic Revolution, and as I learned more of the revolution, I was attracted to its ideals, the uprising of the oppressed, the opposition to American imperialism (the Great Satan), the government of the righteous jurists and the rejection of the world order imposed on developing countries by arrogant European powers and their surrogates. These messages found a receptive heart and an open mind—a heart that had been conditioned by what Malcolm X referred to as the American nightmare and a mind that was thoroughly leftist.

Speaking of Malcolm X, my first significant public speech—the first of hundreds if not thousands—was about Malcolm X, at a program organized by the Jamāt in Baltimore, Maryland. People liked the talk, and gradually I found myself speaking more and more at various venues. I would complete my studies in International Relations at the American University, graduating cum laude, and go on to complete a Masters degree in political science at Rutgers University in New Jersey, studying in an extremely leftist department.

During my time in New Jersey, I continued to be active in Islām, co-founding Masjid[3] al-Hudā, which exists in New Brunswick to this day. I was also active in doing anti-drug work, from an Islāmic perspective, in many of the area housing projects. It was also in New Brunswick that I was exposed to the Salafī movement. A number of area Muslims had been influenced by a Lebanese Salafī activist by the name of ᶜAbdullāh Mekāwī. I was essentially a Ḥanafī by default, having learned most of my Islām in Turkey. There the dominant juridical school is that of Abū Ḥanīfa. The individual who introduced me to the Salafī methodology had spent time overseas studying, was fluent in Arabic, and essentially bludgeoned me into submission. I didn't go without a fight, oftentimes ridiculing the docile, pro-American Islām of Saudi Arabia; the headquarters, if you will, for the Salafī call.

I did not realize it at the time, but my being torn between an Iranian-based radicalism and a Saudi-based Salafism mirrored a struggle that was going on in many parts of the Muslim world. The ongoing Iran-Iraq war, in which the Saudis and Kuwaitis were the Iraqis' principal financiers, only exacerbated that struggle. I would go on to embrace the Salafī approach, though in reality, I was never a good Salafī—I was too much of a political activist. This brings up a very important point. The overwhelming majority of Salafīs, owing to the influence of Sheikh Nāṣiriddīn al-Albānī, one of the key figures in the history of the movement, are against any form of political violence. They are a nonpolitical group, so much so that they are often ridiculed by members of other Islāmic organizations. Their emphasis is on purifying the community through the elimination of blameworthy innovations (*bidᶜa*), and instilling a firm adherence to what they understand to be the creed of the early generations of Muslims. While it is certainly true that the overwhelming majority of Jihādists are Salafist in their approach to Islām, they are a small minority at odds with the mainstream Salafīs. Hence, it is unjust to make Salafīs, per se, one of the focal points in the ongoing "terror" war.

When I finished my Masters, I spent a year in Cairo studying Arabic. That was a pivotal year. I had applied to go to the Islāmic University of Madīna in Saudi Arabia before leaving for Cairo. My acceptance letter was delayed, not arriving until I had already departed for Cairo, where I would spend the coming year. When I learned of my acceptance, I decided to stay in Cairo, even though everyone in the circle I was in encouraged me to move on to Madīna. My decision not to leave was fateful. Had I gone, I would have likely become a very influential caller to the Salafī way in America, although God knows best. A good friend of mine was also accepted and went on to become one of the few African American graduates of that influential institution and a leading caller to the Salafī path. As for myself, I would remain on the fringes of the movement.

Upon returning to America, I reestablished residence in Connecticut, settling in New Haven, where two of my brothers and sisters were then residing. I would soon participate in co-founding Masjid al-Islām. I became the Imām (spiritual leader) of the mosque. For the next six years, our mosque would be the most politically active mosque in America, in my estimation. We were constantly mobilizing the believers for trips to New York to participate in demonstrations related to various Islāmic causes. When Imām Sirāj Wahhāj closed the crack houses in Brooklyn, we had brothers going down to participate in the overnight patrols. When we launched our own mini "war" against the drug dealers in New Haven, we had Arabs, Pakistanis, Malaysians, Africans, and European converts—men and women joining us in middle of the ghetto, in the middle of the night—standing between drug pushers and their customers. We were active in the schools, initiating drug-free zones around schoolyards and providing instructors to participate in after-school programs for the children of working mothers. We also provided volunteers to patrol housing projects that were being devastated by the violence that accompanied the crack epidemic of the late 1980s and early 1990s.

We also had a very active propagation program. At our peak, we had two local access television programs airing every week. I had a periodic column in the *New Haven Register*, Connecticut's second largest daily newspaper. We sponsored numerous programs at various venues in the city, and there was seldom a program sponsored by any other organizations or groups at which our mosque was not represented. I always maintain that if someone had given us a million dollars, we could have taken over the city.

At the time, my views on Islām were deeply influenced by my life experience and my political education. I held and expounded some radical views. These have been most widely highlighted in an infamous pamphlet I wrote entitled, *Muslim Participation in the American Political Process.*[4] In that work, I personally advocated political non-participation and elaborated why in the treatise. However, I never categorically condemned participation. To quote from the introduction to the work,

> Owing to the complexity of the American political process, it would be extremely difficult for an alert Muslim to issue either a blanket condemnation or approval of a Muslim involving himself in that process. Any given aspect of that process would have to be analyzed individually in order to ascertain with any degree of accuracy its compatibility with Islāmic principles and practices. Despite this fact, many Muslims engage in a headlong rush to either uncritically involve themselves in politics—oftentimes priding themselves in their political maturity and sophistication; while others rush with equal enthusiasm to condemn such involvement, usually basing their decision on overly simplistic arguments.

> The purpose of this paper is to avoid either of those two extremes. While not outright condemning involvement in the political process in this country, we urge extreme caution and consideration before Muslims engage themselves in it.[5]

I further stated in the conclusion,

> We are not trying to discourage Muslims from any level of political work. We have not been deluded into believing that this humble work constitutes a definitive statement on the subject of systemic political involvement. We have been asked to prepare this paper for a seminar to be held in September of 1992, and have hastily responded. Many of the ideas expressed herein will have to be clarified and developed further.[6]

Despite these and other qualifications throughout the work, quotes from it have been taken out of context and used to render the work a sort of Muslim "Communist Manifesto." My intention was merely to participate in a discussion.

One of the greatest sources of our strength at Masjid al-Islām was our devotional program. During the last ten days of Ramaḍān, many of the families in the community would spend the night in the mosque in worship. The children would be put to sleep in a separate room, and the believers would head for the prayer hall. We would complete four thirtieths of the Qur'ān during the prayers of those nights, one thirtieth during the units of the special Ramaḍān (*Tarāwīḥ*) prayer and one thirtieth during each of the three units of the even (*shāfʿī*) and odd (*witr*) prayers. We had frequent spiritual retreats, usually renting a conference center on the Connecticut coastline and spending the weekend hiking, exercising, reading the Qur'ān, engaging in religious instruction, and reciting litanies—which we would often do in groups, even though we had neither knowledge of nor inclination towards Sufism. This latter practice is an example of my being a lax Salafī. We read through the *Gardens of the Righteous* (*Riyāḍ aṣ-Ṣāliḥīn*) twice, from cover to cover, after the night prayer (*ʿIshā'*), once with the commentary of Dr. Muṣṭafā Bughā, as well as other texts. The emphasis was always on implementing what we were reading.

During the time I was serving as Imām of Masjid al-Islām, I was also teaching political science as an adjunct professor at Southern Connecticut State University. I enjoyed great popularity among the students, so much so that my contract was renewed on a semester basis for six consecutive years. I was even offered a full-time position if I completed my Ph.D. I made an abortive attempt to do just that, enrolling for a year in a doctoral program at the University of Connecticut. However, I was too deeply involved in the community to give that effort its full right.

Despite the success of Masjid al-Islām, I increasingly realized the limitations of my personal knowledge of the religion. This realization was heightened when I obtained a copy of Sheikh Nūḥ Ḥā Mīm Keller's translation of *Reliance of the Traveler*[7] in 1993. Perusing the pages of that manual helped me realize that as Muslims we are heirs of a rich intellectual heritage and that if we are to contribute to the perpetuation of that heritage and to the advancement of human civilization, we are going to have to master it. In 1994, I made the difficult decision to leave the mosque, leave the university, and go to Syria to study Islām.

It was in Syria that I discovered my humanity. As I saw it, my mother was right in her assessment of our neighbor who had joined the Nation of Islām. True manhood was not to be found in an ideology, and I had been approaching Islām as an ideology. It was to be found, as she expressed it, in "coming to grips with life as a human being." Being removed from the racial tension that characterizes American life—which, to a greater or lesser extent, works to dehumanize us all—and being in the company of righteous men and women who had worked consciously and scrupulously for years to refine their true humanity enabled me to see my own. It was during those years in Syria that I was also able to transcend what I saw as the narrowness of the Salafī approach to Islām and come into a fuller and richer religious expression.

Being in a lineage-conscious Arab society made me conscious of my own unknown roots. Filling out various applications at the school I was enrolled in, I would write, in Arabic, Zaid Shākir. The question would invariably arise, "Zaid Shākir, the son of whom?" "Zaid Shākir the son of Donald." "Who is Donald the son of?" Here the dialogue would end. I did not know my paternal grandfather's name. This sad reality made me think deeply about my ancestors whose lives had been shaped, either as victors or victims, by the American saga. My personal history was part of that saga, and I had no other place to call home. That reality was further reinforced by another part of the application process. After my name was finally recorded, the epithet *al-Amrīkī* (the American) was added. That being the case, as a Muslim, I came to see that I had an obligation to try to make the land of my birth better. I believe that my work as a Muslim, prior to even going to Syria, had done just that. It had helped to make America just a little better. However, that betterment was a residual consequence of my Islāmic work, not a purposeful goal.

Another insight gained from my time in Syria occurred during the frequent visits to the family of a fellow student in the city of Ḥamā. A large part of that extremely religious city was destroyed during a brutally repressed rebellion that occurred there during early 1981. Upwards of 30,000 people, almost all of them unarmed civilians, had been massacred in the process. Visiting the city over fifteen years later, the devastation was still evident. That devastation was not just the physical destruction to be seen in the affected neighborhoods—looted museums, gutted buildings, and the holes and imprints of bullets, tank shells, and artillery rounds—but also in the faces of the widows, widowers, and orphans. It was similarly evident in the frustration and pain of wives and children whose husbands and fathers were still languishing in a distant prison, with no opportunity for even the briefest visit.

I had frequently and irresponsibly talked about revolution—Islāmic revolution—during my days at Masjid al-Islām. Here I got to see up close the human cost of a real revolution. Ḥamā is an all-Muslim city. In Syria 80% of the population is Sunnī Muslim. The Sunnī revolutionaries were ruthlessly crushed. What would be the fate of the 3% Muslim population of the United States if a cadre of confused individuals was to attempt such an uprising in America? Long before the tragic events of September 11, 2001, the word revolution, and a lot of other Marxist rhetoric, as I assessed it, started disappearing from my Islāmic vocabulary.

Another consequence of my time in Syria was the demystification of the Muslim world. I no longer viewed it as a mythical place where an ideal Islām was practiced. It was now a real human society with real human problems, and a lot of those problems made certain aspects of American society start to look really good—the crass rudeness of many of the common folk, the doggish disrespect many of the men displayed towards even pious foreign women, the inability of people to stand in a line and respect the rights of those who had been waiting longer than they had, and an insane obsession with white skin. In myriad ways, I was forced to reassess my view of American society.

Certainly, America still has her problems, not the least of which is a nagging racism that informs many things from foreign policy decisions to accepting the public denigration of Islām and Muslims; a situation which under the right circumstances may lead to pogroms the likes of which this country has not witnessed since the immediate aftermath of Reconstruction in the South. However, there is still a lot of potential that provides the basis for a desire to serve the people here, rather than hate them.

Upon leaving Syria, I returned to New Haven in late 2001 to resume my work at Masjid al-Islām. However, much had changed, including myself. The chemistry that had previously existed was gone, shattered by the migrations, divisions, and divorces that ravaged the community during my time overseas. After 18 months, I would move on to join the staff at Zaytuna Institute, founded by a dear friend, Shaykh Ḥamza Yūsuf, to work to advance what I saw as a balanced, tradition-respecting Islām; an Islām conducive to bringing forth the humanity we so desperately seek as we grope along as a society into this new century.

They say that travel broadens ones horizons, and with age comes wisdom. Mine has been a long journey that has now spanned nearly half a century. I have been blessed to be close to many of the trends and events shaping today's headlines. Hopefully, the length and duration of my journey has bequeathed unto me enough experience and wisdom to make these words beneficial to those I am fortunate enough to share them with. If they serve that purpose, I praise and thank God.

Notes

1. Richelene Mitchell, *Dear Self*, unpublished manuscript, 240.
2. Mitchell, 225.
3. Masjid is the Arabic word for mosque.
4. Imām Zaid Shākir, *Muslim Participation in the American Political Process* (New Haven, CT: New Islamic Directions, 1992).
5. Shākir, 1.
6. Shākir, 10.
7. Nūḥ Ḥā Mīm Keller, *The Reliance of the Traveler: A Classical Manual of Islamic Sacred Law* (Dubai: Modern Printing Press, 1991).

We Are All Collateral Damage

THE ROADS TO PEACE

The roads to peace are paths of war.
The gentle dove will leave her scar.
The moral men to say the least,
will kill us all to get their peace.
The roads that lead to victories gained,
are filled with people full of pain.
Only our Creator knew,
we'd kill so many to save so few.

The recent terrorist tragedy in London is disheartening. Once again some nefarious force has seen fit to totally disregard innocent human life in pursuit of a vile agenda that few of us know and even fewer can understand. The response of the world leaders assembled in Edinburgh for the G-8 Summit is perhaps more disheartening, as it promises more of the misguided policies that have proven so ineffective in prosecuting the war on terror. The leaders of the Western powers continue to imply that they will fight violence with more violence of their own. If current events are any indicator of future developments, such a policy will only serve to beget yet more terrorism.

This is a war being guided on both sides by self-righteous murderers whose motives and proclamations mirror each other. Each side sees God as being exclusively with it. The restraint and judiciousness urged by Christian and Islamic theology to guide the execution of war is cast aside with wanton impunity. Each side manipulates a vulnerable public to create a climate that allows for the perpetuation and the inevitable escalation of the ongoing slaughter. Each side reserves the right to use the spectacle of indiscriminate violence to "Shock and Awe" the opposition, yet will deny that its tactics can be described as terrorism. Each side sees its civilian population as hapless, innocent victims, while the suffering innocent civilians on the other side are acceptable collateral damage.

There will never be any real progress in ending this terror war until we realize that we have all become collateral damage, unacceptable collateral damage. There is no *they* or *we* in this affair, *we* are *they* and *they* are *we*. When a child in New York never sees his mother again because she was crushed in a collapsed tower at the World Trade Center, we all have suffered an irreplaceable loss. When an impoverished family in Afghanistan is bombed from the face of the Earth by a misguided missile, something of our collective humanity is destroyed by the blast. When a child in Iraq is born with gross birth defects due to his mother's exposure to depleted uranium, we have all been deformed. When commuters in London fear ever again entering the Underground because of the ill-advised actions of a handful of desperate fanatics, their insecurity touches us all.

We, the collaterally damaged, will continue to exist in a state of dehumanizing loss, deformity, and insecurity until we rise up, unite, and refuse to support at any level the policies of leaders who continually fail to heed one of the surest of all political lessons: killing innocent civilians will never lead to a positive outcome for the transgressing party. This realization is the first meaningful salvo anyone could fire in a real war on terror. However, as long as we are not as moved by the suffering of innocent civilians anywhere as we are by the suffering of those close to us, it will be a salvo that remains unfired.

Abraham's Story عليه السلام

The story of Pilgrimage (*Ḥajj*) and the feast (*ʿĪd*) that accompanies it focuses our attention on the story of Abraham عليه السلام. God mentions the origins of the Pilgrimage when He orders Abraham عليه السلام, *Proclaim the Pilgrimage to all of humanity; they will respond, coming [to the Sacred House] on foot, riding every possible conveyance, coming from every distant path.* [22:27] It is related that Abraham عليه السلام responded by saying, "My Lord! How can I call all of humanity when my voice will not carry that far?" God said, "Issue the call, and We will make your voice reach them." Abraham عليه السلام then stood at his station (*Maqām*) and proclaimed, "O People! Your Lord has established a house of worship, make pilgrimage onto it!" It is then related that God caused the mountains to bow low in humility, and Abraham's voice عليه السلام traveled to the far corners of the Earth. Every animate and inanimate creation, along with those who had been decreed to make the Pilgrimage until the Day of Resurrection, then proclaimed, "We are responding in your dutiful service, O God! We are responding (*Labbaykallāhumma Labbayk*)!"[1]

In choosing Abraham عليه السلام to make that awesome call, God honored him greatly. He further honored him with one of the most profound descriptions ever given to a human being. He says, *Truly Abraham was a nation, devoutly obedient to God. Naturally inclining towards the true faith, he was not amongst the idolaters. He was abundantly thankful for the blessings [God] bestowed upon him. He chose him, and guided him to a Straight Way.* [16:120-121]

God describes Abraham ﷺ as a nation. The exegetes mention many possible interpretations for this expression. One interpretation is that he was a repository of all good human traits and virtues. During his long and distinguished life, Abraham ﷺ demonstrated characteristics such as chivalry, patience, honesty, loyalty, hospitality, graciousness, and most importantly, an uncompromising commitment to upholding the Oneness of God. As he was, so should we be. We should exert our utmost to embody these and other prophetic virtues. Furthermore, we should realize that it is our duty to call humanity to these virtues. God orders us, *Let there arise from you a community calling to all that is good.* [3:104]

Another interpretation of the expression "Abraham was a nation..." is that he was an upright leader whose example is to be followed. Similarly, the Islāmic community should be an exemplar for all of humanity. God, Exalted is He, describes our community in the following terms, *You are the best community raised up for the benefit of humanity. You enjoin what is right, you forbid what is wrong, and you believe in God.* [3:110]

The challenge of exemplifying the prophetic virtues, coupled with the challenge of calling humanity to those virtues, requires that we rise to the challenge of leadership. Meeting that challenge will require a vastly enhanced base of both religious and worldly knowledge in our communities. Collectively, our entire community—men, women, and youth—has to aspire to heightened levels of educational attainment. As John Kennedy, Malcolm X, and many others have said, "knowledge is power." We cannot deceive ourselves into thinking that we are in a position to even begin to lead humanity. To meet the challenge of leadership, we must meet the challenge of enhanced education and literacy.

This challenge is especially pressing for our religious leaders. Contributing to the solution to problems related to global development and population growth—medical crises such as AIDS and SARS, bioethical issues such as human stem cell research, cloning, and vivisection, as well as other contentious religious, philosophical, social, political, cultural, and economic issues—will require scholars who are steeped in our intellectual tradition, conversant with contemporary intellectual currents, and capable of judiciously assessing controversial situations. It will also require scholars who have a deep relationship with God, or to use the traditional appellation, *ᶜUlamā' ᶜĀmilīn*. As Ibn ᶜAṭā'Allāh relates in his aphorisms, "Nothing you seek relying on your Lord will ever be difficult. And nothing you seek relying on yourself will ever be easy."[2]

As the Arabs say, "One lacking something cannot give it to others." If we lack knowledge of the vastness of our intellectual heritage, especially its jurisprudential principles and rulings, we will continue to be bogged down in unnecessary arguments and disputes which only serve to waste valuable time, sap vital energy, and create sometimes irreconcilable animosity and enmity in our ranks. If we continue to lack adequate knowledge of the world—its prevailing social, political, and economic systems; its prevailing religious, intellectual, and philosophical schools; and its prevailing cultural trends—then our ability to formulate a meaningful, constructive critique of those systems and schools will be greatly hampered, if not hamstrung.

Rising to this challenge will require a broad vision and tremendous courage on our part. Part of the broad vision needed by our scholars will involve having the ability to transcend current academic modalities and methodologies. Traditionally-trained scholars frequently hear from their university-trained counterparts how important it is to move beyond the analytical limitations imposed by "fossilized" curricula, anachronistic methodologies, and a stultifying formalism. While such advice is well founded, those whose training has been in the western academy should realize that in order to maximize their benefit to our community, they will have to transcend the constraints imposed by work in the average academic department. The departmentalization of knowledge facilitates research, but does little to enhance our understanding of the many nuances and complexities present in a human society. An interdisciplinary approach to knowledge acquisition will probably prove more fruitful in an effort to gain more socially relevant insights. However, the ultimate goal of our young scholars should be the creation of a non-disciplinary paradigm. Such a paradigm would surely be more reflective of the phenomena it attempts to explain.

In trying to break away from linear research methodologies strongly influenced by the philosophy of science, a discipline itself greatly influenced by physics, our young university-trained intellectuals will have to have the courage to creatively challenge reigning paradigms and the constantly narrowing focus of research. Herman Daley suggests that the computer has made it possible for physicists to develop new models whose complexity opens up what was once one of the narrowest of fields to new and exiting interdisciplinary research modalities.[3] Perhaps our new generation of scholars can build on those insights and engage in research that allows us to creatively use Islāmic studies and the social sciences to rigorously address the plethora of problems plaguing our Islāmic communities and humanity at large.

Our young scholars will also have to have an a priori commitment to serve the public. American intellectual life has been radically transformed during the past half century. Before that transformation, the greatest minds in the fields of religion, politics, society, culture, and economics wrote in a vernacular that was accessible to the general reading public. Their ideas helped to shape both popular and political culture. The ideas of Reinhold Niebuhr, Daniel Bell,

John Kenneth Galbraith, C. Wright Mills, Lewis Mumford, and Michael Harrington, for example, were not only made available in the very readable volumes they authored, they were also disseminated in the leading periodicals of the day: *Harper's, The Atlantic Monthly, The New Yorker*, and *The Saturday Evening Post.*

Today, intellectuals are generally content to be academics, and as academics they exist in a world divorced from the world inhabited by the public intellectuals of the past. As Russell Jacoby writes:

> To put it sharply: the habitat, manners, and idiom of intellectuals have been transformed within the past fifty years. Younger intellectuals no longer need or want a larger public; they are almost exclusively professors. Campuses are their homes; colleagues are their audiences; monographs and specialized journals their media.[4]

He further notes:

> Academics write for professional journals that, unlike the little magazines, create insular societies. The professors share an idiom and a discipline. Gathering in annual conferences to compare notes, they constitute their own universe. A "famous" sociologist or art historian means famous to other sociologists and art historians, not to anyone else. As intellectuals became academics, they had no need to write in public prose; they did not, and finally they could not.[5]

The situation Jacoby describes would not be a cause for alarm, were it not for the fact that the effective divorcing of intellectuals from public life has had a devastating effect on popular culture and politics. The current crassness which defines American popular culture and political discourse can surely be attributed, in part, to the lack of meaningful, accessible public intellectuals. If we Muslims are to reinvigorate our culture and our socio-political discourse, we will have to encourage and make a real space for the vital input of our intellectuals. For their part, those intellectuals will have to step forward and fill that space.

This call should in no way be seen as an appeal to our young intellectuals to lower their standards. Furthermore, in pointing to the example of intellectuals who were considered at the height of their respective disciplines yet possessed the ability to address the general public, we need not point to the likes of Daniel Bell. In our tradition, we have figures like Imām al-Ghazālī. He was not only able to master and refute, in their language, the arguments of the most advanced philosophers and logicians of his age, he was also able to express complex theological ideas and issues in terms readily accessible to and accepted by ordinary Muslims in works such as his *Revival of the Religious Sciences.*[6]

Abraham عليه السلام is described as being devoutly, and unflinchingly obedient to God. God says in the Qur'ān that he was *Devoutly Obedient...* [16:120] The believers are also noted for their strict obedience—among other characteristics. God describes them as *Those who are steadfastly patient, exceedingly honest, devoutly obedient, selflessly charitable, those who invoke the Forgiveness of God during the last reaches of the night.* [3:17] Abraham عليه السلام and all of the devout servants of this community are people who obey God whether it is easy or difficult, whether they personally incline towards a certain act or not, whether they are in a state of security or fear, whether they are experiencing abundance or deprivation. True worship and devotion are unconditional.

Abraham عليه السلام, a strict monotheist, was naturally inclined towards the worship of God. The magnitude of this characteristic is brought home to us when we realize that Abraham عليه السلام was alone in a world of idolatry. Despite that, he was prepared to sacrifice his life to defend and uphold the standard of the Oneness of God. In his days, the idols that people worshipped were idols of wood and stone. Today, the idols people worship have changed. However, we should be opposed to idol worship nonetheless, especially when that worship, in its modern manifestations, is proving extremely destructive to individuals and societies.

The modern and postmodern conditions have bequeathed unto humanity an array of "idols" that are worshipped besides God. Perhaps the greatest idol arising from our condition is the individual's worship of himself. In what sociologist Christopher Lasch describes as a "culture of narcissism,"[7] it is easy to appreciate the penetrating question asked by God in the Qur'ān, *Have you not seen one who has taken his vain inclinations as his god?* [45:23]

The havoc being wreaked on the western psyche and soul by a pervasive narcissism is beginning to manifest itself in our Muslim homelands. Much of that damage can be traced to the pervasiveness of western culture, a pervasiveness that has not emerged from a congruent belief and social system. In other words, what we see in our Muslim homelands is the tree of western culture grafted onto Islāmic roots. Such a graft is destined to produce the sort of societal dysfunction and anomie we have seen prevailing in most Muslim countries.

We can see the extent of the pervasiveness of western culture in our lands when we consider that the political institutions that guide even Islāmic movements and self-proclaimed Islāmic governments are western institutions. We fight our battles using western military technology and tactics. We are educated in institutions patterned after those in the West. Increasingly, most of our urban populations are housed in western-styled, cement apartment blocs. We wear western clothing. We cultivate our lands according to western agricultural techniques. We work in western-styled factories—usually subsidiaries of western multinationals. Those of us who can afford to do so eat in western restaurants such as McDonalds, Kentucky Fried Chicken, or local imitations of the same. We spend billions of dollars smoking and cultivating tobacco, a destructive habit popularized in the West. We spend greater billions on soft drinks, even when it affects our ability to purchase food and drink of real nutritional value for our families. We bring our sick to hospitals built and administered according to western models, utilizing western medicines and surgical techniques. We squander valuable time watching meaningless programs on television sets pioneered in the West, when not reading newspapers that utilize western journalistic techniques and advertising practices or playing sports developed in the West. We relax to what is essentially western music, even though for the time being, most of the lyrics are still in our eastern tongues. Even our intelligentsia is unified by western languages, English or French, and not Arabic. In such a cultural milieu, it would be difficult to expect that Islām would have a deep impact on the lives of ordinary people.

We do not intend for this address to become an irresponsible diatribe against the West. However, many of the problems facing humanity, such as crushing national debts, grinding poverty, growing disparities between the rich and the poor, the continued and accelerating destruction of the environment, and our exponentially enhanced ability to kill each other with increasingly sophisticated and deadly weaponry, are facilitated by an international environment shaped by increasingly hegemonic western institutions. As Muslims, we should have the vision and courage—Abrahamic courage—to work for a world that, while acknowledging and benefiting from the many positive advancements bequeathed to humanity by western materialist civilization, minimizes the damage caused by its negative and darker innovations.

Abraham عليه السلام was also described as being grateful for the many gifts and blessings bestowed upon him by God. We read in the Qur'ān, *He [Abraham] was abundantly grateful for the blessings [God] bestowed upon him.* [16:120-121] Graciousness should have an exalted place in the life of every Muslim, especially here in America. In terms of material blessings, we have more to thank God for than any other group of Muslims on earth. More than any other group of Muslims, we have experienced the fullness of the meaning conveyed by the following verse: *He has completed His Blessings upon you, in open and hidden ways.* [31:20] Were we to attempt to enumerate or express the magnitude of those blessings, we would be unable to do so. Among the open blessings we could mention include food, drink, potable water, sanitation, health, wealth, shelter, clothing, security, and the fact that, despite certain well-publicized abuses, the overwhelming majority of us lives under the protection of the law. Among the hidden blessings, we could mention education, understanding, discernment, psychological stability, and faith—the greatest blessing of all.

All of these blessings and countless others we could mention are subordinate to two other blessings that are frequently completely taken for granted: the blessing of existence and the blessing of sustentation. Ibn ʿAṭā'Allāh expresses the immensity of those blessings in the following penetrating words, "[There are] two blessings that are not extraneous to anything in existence and that are indispensable for every form of creation: the blessing of origination and the blessing of sustentation."[8] No matter what heights of arrogance and ingratitude a human being may reach, there is no one who will go so far as to claim that he has brought himself into existence or that she sustains her own life.

Therefore, we should fervently and without stint express our gratitude to our Lord. Imām al-Ghazālī mentions that graciousness consists of knowledge, a state, and action. As for knowledge, it is a firm knowledge of the One who bestows all gifts (God). As for the state, it is the delight which ensues because of His (God's) bestowing the gift. As for the action, it is undertaking that which is sought and beloved by God; namely, pure, unadulterated worship and devotion.[9]

So let us go forward and rededicate ourselves to the worship of God and the service of humanity. Let us thank God for the many blessings He has bestowed upon us with every ounce of energy we can muster, from the bottom of our hearts and from the depths of our soul.

Let us also remember, that God does nothing in vain. Our being Muslim at this critical juncture in history is not without purpose. Our existence here in this country is part of a divine plan, and the deeper our understanding of that plan, the deeper our realization of the tremendous responsibility we shoulder. Our situation presents us with staggering challenges and places before us daunting work. However, if we take up those challenges with the courage, determination, vision, and patience that availed Abraham عليه السلام throughout his life, like him, we may be blessed to change the course of history.

Notes

1 For the full details of this event, see Ibn Kathīr, *Tafsīr al-Qur'ān al-ᶜAẓīm* (Beirut, Ṣaydā: al-Maktaba al-ᶜAṣriyya, 1416 AH/1996 CE), 3:204.

2 ᶜAbd al-Majīd ash-Sharnūbī, *Sharḥ al-Ḥikam al-ᶜAṭā'iyya* (Damascus: Dār ibn Kathīr, 1413 AH/1992 CE), 38:35.

3 See Herman Daly and John B. Cobb, Jr., *For the Common Good:Redirecting the Economy Towards Community, the Environment, and a Sustainable Future* (Boston: Beacon Press, 1994), 363-366.

4 Russell Jacoby, *The Last Intellectuals: American Culture in the Age of Academe* (New York: Basic Books, 1987), 6.

5 Jacoby, 7.

6 Abū Ḥamīd al-Ghazālī, *Iḥyā' ᶜUlūm ad-Dīn* (Beirut: Dār al-Qutayba, 1412 AH/1992 CE).

7 This term has been popularized by Lasch's book, *The Culture of Narcissism: American Life in an Age of Diminishing Expectations* (New York: W.M. Horton & Company, 1979).

8 Ash-Sharnūbī, 83, no. 97.

9 Al-Ghazālī, 4:120.

Islām and the Question of Nationalism[1]

The nation-state, which involves wedding a specific people to a sovereign territorial entity, is a modern phenomenon. For example, the unity of the Italian city-states into a coherent modern nation-state did not occur until the late 1850s. The unification of Germany under Prussia did not occur until 1871. Even though there were many French kingdoms, and even a French empire under Napoleon, it could be argued that the emergence of France as a viable, modern nation-state did not occur before Jules Ferry established universal public education during the 19th century. Outside of Europe, excluding European settler states such as America and with the notable exception of Japan, one can not meaningfully discuss the existence of viable nation-states until the 20th century.

Nationalism, the movement of a people to establish an autonomous state, a phenomenon instrumental in the creation of the contemporary international system, is also strictly modern. It can be seen as part of a 19th century European reaction—a political offspring of Romanticism—to the universalizing and anti-authoritarian tendencies of the earlier Enlightenment. There are, however, elements of nationalist thought that are extremely ancient. Most of these, such as an exclusivist, chauvinistic attachment to a particular group and the sacrificing of universal human concerns on the altar of particularistic national interests, are strongly rejected by Islām. It is from this point of departure that we can develop a credible Islāmic critique of nationalism.

Islām, the last of the Abrahamic religions, has been defined as "submission to the will of God," also, "the state of peace resulting from submitting to the will of God," and "acknowledging, then being led by everything brought by the Prophet Muḥammad ﷺ." One of the distinguishing features of Islām, emphasized in the last definition, is its comprehensiveness. The way of life it informs has been viewed as touching on every aspect of human existence.

This comprehensiveness can be gleaned from a cursory view of most expansive Islāmic law manuals. For example, in the introduction to a contemporary work on the jurisprudence of the Shāfiʿī school, the authors mention the following seven basic areas covered by Islāmic Law:

1. Worship (al-ʿIbādah): prayer, fasting, etc.
2. Family Matters (al-Aḥwāl al-Shakhsiyya): marriage, divorce, inheritance, etc.
3. Interpersonal Relations (al-Muʿāmalāt): buying, selling, legal claims, etc.
4. Duties and Responsibilities of the Political Governors and the Governed (al-Aḥkām al-Sulṭaniyya): establishing justice, preventing oppression, rights of obedience, etc.
5. Criminal Justice and Maintaining Public Order (al-Ḥudūd): punishing thieves, adulterers, maintaining safety, etc.
6. Political Relations (al-Siyar): war, peace, truces, etc.
7. Character Reformation and Good Manners (al-Akhlāq wa'l-Ādāb): abstention, patience, humility, courage, etc.[2]

Since nationalism, as stated, is a modern phenomenon, it has not been explicitly dealt with in any of the aforementioned areas.

However, as we will attempt to show, Islām contains teachings which clearly argue against elements of nationalist thought. It also argues against the chauvinism and exclusiveness which the nationalist project engenders. These phenomena are a major part of what we will call the nationalist question. In this article, we will attempt to critically examine the nationalist question in light of fundamental Islāmic teachings. That examination will begin with a section that examines Islāmic teachings of relevance in examining that question, followed by a section that defines nationalism rigorously and then analyzes it in the light of Islāmic teachings. Although this arrangement will involve a degree of redundancy, it will hopefully make the overall discussion more meaningful for those not familiar with the Islāmic concepts we introduce initially. Finally, we will conclude the article with some reflections on the role Islām can play in our efforts to move beyond nationalism.

Nationalist Concepts in the Light of Islām

Islām posits that humanity shares a common ancestry. God says in the Qur'ān, *O Mankind! We have created you from a single pair, a male and female, then made you into nations and tribes in order that you come to know one another [not that you may despise one another]. The most honored of you with God is the most pious. And God is Well Informed, Knowledgeable.* [49:13] He also says, *O mankind! Be mindful of your Lord who has created you from a single soul, and created from that soul its mate, and has brought forth from them multitudes of men and women.* [4:1] Humanity, as these verses emphasize, has a common ancestry, which creates inseparable bonds of brotherhood and sisterhood between us. Islām, in this regard, does not sanction any scheme that negates or trivializes those bonds, as occurs with conflicting nationalisms.

Islām advocates the essential equality, human worth, and dignity of all people. God says, *We have ennobled the human being.* [17:70]

Similarly, *And their Lord accepted their prayer, and answered them, I will never allow to be lost the work of any of you, be he male or female, you are from one another.* [3:195] These and similar verses emphasize that the fundamental worth of all humans transcends race and gender divisions. Understanding this equality is central if we are to gain a true understanding of how Islām approaches the issue of nationalism. While recognizing the validity of national, racial, tribal, ethnic, and cultural differences, Islām views them as signs of God's creative power, not as the basis for the creation of mutually destructive political agendas.

As for culture and race, God says, *And among His Signs is the creation of Heaven and Earth, and the variation of your languages and your colors. Surely, in this are signs for those endowed with knowledge.* [30:22] We mention this verse here because of our belief that language is the most important element in any cultural system. Hence, it is one of the strongest bases of national identity.

Islām also acknowledges that distinct people, nations, and tribes can be vested with unique historical missions. God says, *The Romans have been defeated in a nearby land. However, despite this defeat of theirs, they will soon be victorious within a few years. And with God is the Command, in the past and the future. And on that day, the believers will rejoice.* [30: 2-4] The point here is that God decreed this victory for the Romans as a people. Their historical destiny as a people was to defeat the Persians. Conversely, the Persians, after their initial triumph, were destined to be defeated by the Romans in the end. He also says, concerning the idea of distinct nations, *Every nation has a fixed term. When that term expires, they can neither delay nor hasten [their inevitable demise].* [7:34]

This idea of distinct historical missions is further born out by the fact that nations, prior to the advent of the prophecy of Muḥammad ﷺ, were addressed by prophets sent specifically to them.

Noah (*Nūḥ*) عليه السلام was sent specifically to his people.[3] Hūd عليه السلام was sent specifically to the people of ʿĀd.[4] Sāliḥ عليه السلام was sent to the people of Thamūd.[5] The message of these and other Prophets, Peace of God be upon them all, was directed towards their respective peoples, constituting a divine affirmation of their distinct national identities.

However, one should not be led to believe that the specificity of those prophetic missions, which preceded that of Muḥammad ﷺ, can be used as a justification for pursuing narrow nationalistic agendas. That is because the specificity of those messages was abrogated by the universality of the message of Muḥammad ﷺ. God says, describing that message, *Say to them, [O Muḥammad!], "I am the messenger of God to you all!"* [7:158]

This verse is especially significant in that it occurs after a lengthy description, in *Sūra al-ʿArāf*, of the earlier Prophets and their messages. Consider the previous four citations in that regard. It is as if God is especially emphasizing the universality of the mission of the Prophet Muḥammad ﷺ by presenting it in contradistinction to the earlier messages. It is significant that this transition from specific messages to a universal one occurred at the advent of an era when the overland trade routes, which would be created by the vast, functionally unified Islāmic Empire, would integrate the entirety of the "known" world to an extent unprecedented in history; it came just when the world was prepared to receive such a message.

The universality of that message counters the idea that the division of humans into their respective nations, tribes, cultural and ethnic identity groups, possessors of distinct historical missions, or any other groupings should constitute the basis for the creation of destructive, mutually exclusive, and potentially belligerent agendas. It also rejects the idea of these distinctions being the basis for any claims of superiority. God reminds us that these differences are rooted in the accident of birth. They exist as a means for our mutual recognition of the creative power of God and as a means for us to come to know and appreciate each other.[6] Any claim of superiority can only be based on superior devotion and ethics, bases which transcend the accident of birth. God says in that regard, *The most honored of you with God is the most pious.* [49:13]

Assessing Nationalism

In this part of our article many of the previously-outlined concepts will be revisited in the context of a more rigorous assessment of nationalism from an Islāmic perspective. This assessment will be structured around the following definition of nationalism, namely, "The belief that each nation has both the right and duty to constitute itself as a state."[7] According to this and most other definitions, the essence of nationalism involves the wedding of a nation to a state. However, if we are to understand the dynamics involved in the formation of national identity, the organizational impetus that moves a nation to seek statehood, we need to understand six terms, some of which we have previously mentioned in this article: 1. nation, 2. culture, 3. state, 4. fear, 5. anger, and 6. victimization.

Nation

A nation has been defined as "an historical concept founded on a cultural identity shared by a single people."[8] As mentioned earlier, Islām does not reject the idea of a nation. All of the Prophets before Muḥammad ﷺ were sent to specific nations. However, if that shared identity leads to a scheme where the rights or humanity of other groups are denied by an exclusivist quest for sovereignty, the ensuing nationalist enterprise is questioned by Islām. The reason for that will be clarified towards the end of this article.

Culture

Culture, defined anthropologically and sociologically, "denotes indifferently all manifestations of social life which are not concerned with the reproduction and sustenance of human beings. Thus customs, habits of association, religious observances, even specific beliefs, may be spoken of as part of a culture."[9] Culture is the glue that holds a nation together, for it provides the basis for the tangible distinctions that differentiate one group of people from another. The basic elements of cultural distinction are compatible with Islāmic beliefs. This is illustrated by the following verse in the Qur'ān, *Among His Signs is the creation of Heaven and Earth, and the variation of your languages and your colors. Surely, in this are signs for those endowed with knowledge.* [30:22] This verse, which has been previously referenced, articulates the Islāmic ethos concerning cultural diversity. Diverse cultures, symbolized by varying languages, contribute to the beauty of human society. This diversity is also reflected in the attitude of Islām towards religious diversity, another cultural manifestation. Although Islām can be interpreted as asserting the possession of ultimate truth, it has never negated the right to other forms of religious expression, neither in creed, nor in practice. There are many well-known examples of religious and cultural tolerance in Islāmic history. Perhaps the most frequently cited are the Golden Age of Islāmic Spain[10] and the Ottoman Millet system.[11]

State

The state is a political unit defined in terms of a population, demarcated borders, and an autonomous government.[12] The creation of a state is the ultimate objective of a nationalist movement, in the case of most stateless nations. The potential destructiveness of nationalism is rooted in the fact that most states are nationally heterogeneous and most nations are stateless. If the nationalist aspirations of all people were enthusiastically pursued, a state of perpetual war and severe persecution would probably ensue. Islām anticipates this eventuality and warns against it in unequivocal terms. As we have mentioned earlier in this article, the Qur'ān states that national and ethnic diversity exists *in order that you come to know one another, [not that you despise each other].* [49:13]

Fear

Nationalism involves the effort of a nation to create or maintain an identity with a state. Here our last three terms: fear, anger, and victimization, become relevant. Fear is one of the principle factors motivating a nation to consolidate its control over a particular territory and create a state. Such fear revolves around a real or imagined enemy that is seen as a threat to the existence or interests of a particular nation. Although one of the positive benefits of group solidarity has often been security, when the promise of security is manipulated for political purposes the consequences can be extremely destructive. Such manipulation has inevitably been part of the formula that led to most modern-day genocides.

This security/genocide consanguinity is perhaps best illustrated in the horrific slaughter of Rwanda's Tutsis by the majority Hutus in 1994. Commenting on the propaganda campaign, which preceded and accompanied that genocidal episode, Samantha Power notes, "As genocidal perpetrators so often do as a prelude to summoning the masses, they began claiming the Tutsi were out to exterminate Hutu and appealing for preemptive self-defense."[13] That appeal was answered, resulting in one of the most brutal and intense massacres in modern history.

Islām strives to remove this motivation from human society. We read in the Qur'ān, *Thus does Satan attempt to instill the fear of his dupes into you. Do not fear them. Rather, fear Me, if indeed you are believers.* [3:175] In this verse, God tells the believers not to fear their enemies, rather, to fear Him. And perhaps more importantly, when they establish their political community, to establish it on the fear of God, not on the fear of a real or imagined human adversary, often described in contemporary discourse as the "other." Believers are encouraged to understand that they are united in a human family and that there are fundamental rights accruing to members of that family regardless of their religious affiliations. As mentioned earlier, God has ennobled the human being. This ennoblement precedes the division of humanity into religions, nations, tribes, and other identity groups. At this level of supra-historical existence, all of humanity belongs to a single tribe, the tribe of Ādam ﵇ (*Banī Ādam*).

It is interesting to note that in Islāmic teachings, Satan, who attempts to instill fear of the "other" into human beings, also attempts to base superiority on accidental physical differences. God mentions in the Qur'ān, *What prevented you from prostrating yourself to Ādam when I ordered you to do so? He (Satan) said, "I am better than him. You created me from fire, and you created him from clay."* [7:12] This prototypically racist attitude is reflected in the rhetoric of many bigots, past and present. Satan, blinded by his arrogance, apparently forgot that Ādam's ﵇ distinction lay in the fact that his supposedly low physical origin was augmented by the life spirit (*Rūḥ*), which was breathed into him, and by the fact that God had ennobled him.

The Prophet Muḥammad ﷺ emphasized the fact that physical distinctions are irrelevant in the sight of God. He said, "God does not look at your physical forms, or your wealth. Rather, He looks at your deeds and your hearts."[14] This prophetic tradition argues against using physical distinctions arising from the accident of birth as the basis for any claims of superiority or as the focal point for the creation of chauvinistic movements or states.

Anger and Victimization

Anger is the actualization of fear. In other words, anger is one of the greatest factors urging people to act against the source of their fear. One of the greatest sources of such anger is a feeling of victimization. Ernest Gellner, one of the foremost writers on nationalism, explains the role of victimization in contemporary nationalist thought:

> As the tidal wave of modernization sweeps the world, it makes sure that almost everyone, at some time or another, has cause to feel unjustly treated, and that he can identify the culprits as being of another "nation". If he can also identify enough of the victims as being of the same "nation" as himself, a nationalism is born. If it succeeds, and not all of them can, a nation is born.[15]

As is the case with fear, Islām condemns anger as a motivation for political action. Commenting on the Qur'ānic verse, *When the unbelievers had set up in their hearts the zealotry [for battle], which they had demonstrated during the days of pre-Islāmic ignorance, God sent calm and tranquility upon the Messenger and the believers...* [48:26], Imām al-Ghazālī says, at the beginning of the introduction to a chapter on the condemnation of anger in his famous *Revival of the Religious Sciences*, "The unbelievers are condemned for the unjustified zealotry they manifested due to their anger."[16]

One of the keys to beneficial political decisions, or decisions of any type, is a firm intellectual command. For this reason, Islām expressly forbids a judge from issuing a decision in a state of anger.[17] The previously-cited verse extends this principle into the realm of political action. It was revealed concerning the critical negotiations between the Prophet Muḥammad ﷺ and his Mekkan enemies over the terms of the treaty that was struck at Hudaybiyya. The followers of the Prophet are praised for not letting their anger over the apparently humiliating terms of the treaty distort their better judgment and thereby prevent them from accepting what the Messenger of God ﷺ deemed acceptable. Hence, anger is rejected as a motivation for political action.

Islām also argues against appeals to a sense of victimization as a basis for political action. As opposed to seeking an external culprit or scapegoat to blame one's problems on, Islām encourages individual and group responsibility. God says, in a revealed prophetic tradition:

> Rather it is your actions that I reckon for you. Then I reward you fully for them. Therefore, whoever finds good, let him praise God, and whoever finds other than that, let him blame no one but himself.[18]

The Prophet himself ﷺ said, "Everyone of you is a guardian, and each of you will be asked concerning his/her wards."[19] This cultivation of individual responsibility is so essential in Islām that the person who lacks any wards or possessions is to be reminded of his/her guardianship over his/her very body and to do those divinely sanctioned things that are best for the preservation of that body. Ibn Ḥajar al-ᶜAsqalānī mentions, commenting on the above tradition,

> The single person, who lacks a wife, servant, or child, is responsible for his very limbs, to insure that they implement the commandments and avoid those things which are forbidden in speech, action, and belief. Therefore, his limbs, faculties, and senses are his wards.[20]

These, and similar proof texts, make it clear that Islām wants each individual to take responsibility for his or her actions and to begin to address undesirable situations by seeing how he or she has fallen short in meeting the conditions God has established for the attainment of favorable outcomes in this life. A similar analysis could be made for groups and their collective fates. In a worldly sense, they are responsible for their own uplifting or debasement. God says clearly in this regard, *God does not change the condition of a people until they change the state of their souls.* [13:11]

From this discussion, it should be clear that Islām is against exploiting fear and anger, or cultivating a sense of victimization in order to create the zealousness which pushes a nationalist agenda. It should be noted that this zealousness, which is closely described by what we will term zealous tribal fealty (*ʿAsabiyya*), has been specifically condemned by the Prophet Muḥammad ﷺ. The Prophet ﷺ was asked about zealous tribal fealty. He replied, "It is aiding your folk in [their] oppression."[21] He also said, "One who is killed under the banner of zealous tribal fealty or raises the banner of zealous tribal fealty or aids a party on the basis of zealous tribal fealty, [he/she has died] a death of pre-Islāmic ignorance."[22]

These condemnations by the Prophet ﷺ are aimed at cutting off a dangerous source of disunity and discord in the Muslim ranks. For example, before accepting Islām, the Madinan tribes of al-Aws and al-Khazraj were engaged in long and destructive internecine warfare. Islām united their hearts and joined them politically under one banner. However, on one occasion, their unity was threatened by the effort of a third party to stir up zealous tribal fealty among them. That effort was staved off by the direct intervention of the Prophet ﷺ.[23]

It should be noted here, that the Arabic term *Jāhiliyya* refers to more than the ignorance of the pre-Islāmic Arabs. It also refers to their social, cultural, and political condition. Hence, it includes their practice of burying female newborns alive, their revenge-motivated wars, and other practices. Ibn Manẓūr says, explaining this term,

> It is the state that the Arabs were in prior to Islām. [It refers to] their ignorance of God, be He exalted, His Messenger ﷺ, the laws of the religion, their boasting over their lineage, their arrogance and haughtiness, and other characteristics.[24]

Again, these narrations should make it clear that Islām in no way endorses the idea of mobilizing to pursue an exclusivist political agenda based on tribal or national bonds. Such mobilization, which lies at the heart of the nationalist venture, not only runs counter to clear Islāmic teachings, as we have attempted to show, it has also been the source of many of the most brutal and costly wars in recent history and has manifested itself in all of the genocides that occurred during the 1990s.

The defenders of nationalism, while acknowledging its latent danger, point to its great triumphs, specifically, its role in stopping the advance of the twin totalitarian menaces of Nazism and Stalinist Communism. However, even here, nationalism does not stand above indictment if we view Nazism and Stalinist communism as grotesque manifestations of German and Russian nationalism, respectively.

In the lands of Islām, as has been the case in other parts of the developing world, nationalism has had its most profound impact on western-educated elites. Those elites were instrumental in articulating a post-colonial national consensus. That consensus as to the meaning, purpose, and direction of the post-colonial state was initially greeted with significant mass support throughout the Muslim world. However, the systematic and oftentimes cynical negation of any meaningful mass participation in the political process has led to a widespread view of the nation-state as a foil for self-serving autocratic rule. This perception, coupled with the developmental and strategic failures of the nation-state in the Muslim world, has left many Muslims begging for new forms of political identity and a new basis for political action.

Conclusion

Humanity will not be able to move towards a harmonious state where the actualization of true human unity and our collective security are realities if we do not move beyond the nation-state. Improved means of communication and transportation continue to "shrink" the world. Continuous improvements in weapons technology, conventional and non-conventional, greatly enhance the efficacy of our ability to kill each other. Global problems, such as AIDS, SARS, pollution, and increasingly disastrous economic inequalities, defy unilateral solutions. In light of these and many other pressing facts, we can no longer accept a scheme where, in the words of William Pfaff, "...a nation conceives itself licensed to validate itself by the victimization of another society."[25] Mutual victimization, an unfortunate result of conflicting national interests, creates conditions that could very well lead to our mutual destruction.

That said, nationalism is a reality that lies at the heart of the contemporary global order. Therefore, transcending it will require more than a mere understanding of its inherent dangers. New ways of thinking about the meaning of life, humanity, and human civilization will have to be developed, and new institutions will have to be constructed. Many daunting problems relating to the meaning of national sovereignty, self determination, and citizenship will have to be resolved.

Fortunately, many contemporary developments have already started that process. International finance markets and the real time operations of the largest multinational corporations have already transcended the effective control of individual states. Although these developments currently facilitate oftentimes exploitative and irresponsible corporate behavior, they are part of an evolving global system which could potentially render the nation-state an irrelevant institution.

At the level of the individual citizen, the concept of human rights and the associated phenomenon of humanitarian intervention present additional challenges to the idea of state sovereignty. Human rights imply that the rights owed to individuals supersede the rights that are owed to states. The idea of humanitarian intervention accentuates that conclusion. The sovereignty of the state where such intervention occurs is oftentimes completely bypassed.

These and related developments are forcing a reevaluation of the meaning of national sovereignty in the postmodern world. A similar reevaluation is occurring around the meaning of citizenship in the context of the nation-state. One of the greatest issues in that regard revolves around resolving the challenge of multiculturalism. Of issue here is the political role of collective identities. In other words, how can a privileged majority, in whose interest the state was founded, meaningfully accommodate excluded, disenfranchised, or marginalized minorities. If a meaningful resolution to this issue can be affected within the legal and constitutional framework of individual states, then replicating that solution within the framework of international law should be within the realm of possibility. Both developments, once achieved, will eventually translate into new social and political institutions.

Just as the institutions that facilitated the rise, consolidation, and entrenchment of both nationalism and the nation-state occurred in a distinctive social, cultural, and political milieu—a milieu that was in turn fostered by a distinctive social psychology—a new institutional reality, rooted in its distinctive socio-political culture, will require its own distinctive social psychology. Herein lies the contemporary relevance of Islām. As we have endeavored to demonstrate, Islām provides a set of beliefs and principals that simultaneously foster cultural distinction and universalism. Accommodating these twin developments in an equitable fashion is one of the greatest challenges to be overcome by the emerging globalization of our times.

At the height of its civilization, Islām was able to meet and overcome this challenge by creating a culturally diverse and politically decentralized, yet functionally integrated "global" realm that extended from Spain into China. The fact that an individual such as Ibn Baṭṭūta, the great Moroccan traveler, could go from one end of that realm to another, communicate in a single language (Arabic), and be accepted as a judge in the distant Maldives testifies to the globalization fostered by Islām during that period.[26]

One of the greatest keys to the emergence of that realm was the social psychology fostered by Islām. Perhaps the most important fruit of that social psychology was the creation of a political culture which generally discouraged the development of nationalist thinking. Such a political culture is desperately needed today as many people are beginning to struggle with new forms of transnational organization. If Islām is allowed, by both its enemies and advocates, to contribute to a new global socio-political consensus by helping to resolve the nationalist question, humanity will be well served.

Notes

1 The article is based on a lecture by the same title given by the author at the University of California, Berkeley, in September 2003.

2 Dr. Muṣṭafā al-Bughā, et al., *Al-Fiqh al-Manhajī* (Damascus, Syria: Dār al-ʿUlūm al-Insāniyyah, 1989), 12-13.

3 Al-Qur'ān 7:59.

4 Al-Qur'ān 7:65.

5 Al-Qur'ān 7:73.

6 Al-Qur'ān 49:13.

7 Adam and Jessica Kuper, eds., *The Social Science Encyclopedia* (London, New York: Routledge, 1985), 551.

8 Theodore Couloumbis and James H. Wolfe, *Introduction to International Relations: Power and Justice* (Englewood Cliffs, NJ: Prentice-Hall, Inc., 1978), 37.

9 Roger Scruton, *A Dictionary of Political Thought* (New York, NY: Hill and Wang), 109-110.

10 An excellent study of the culture of tolerance that existed at the height of Islāmic rule in Spain can be found in Maria Menocal's, *Ornament of the World: How Muslims, Jews, and Christians Created a Culture of Tolerance in Medieval Spain* (Boston, New York, London: Little, Brown, and Company, 2002).

11 For a concise, balanced assessment of the nature of the Millet system, see Bernard Lewis, *What Went Wrong: Western Impact and Middle Eastern Response* (Oxford, New York: Oxford University Press, 2002), 33-34.

12 Theodore Columbis and James Wolfe, *Introduction to International Relations: Power and Justice* (Englewood Cliffs, NJ: Prentice-Hall, Inc. 1978), 37.

13 Samantha Power, *A Problem From Hell: America and the Age of Genocide* (New York: Harper Collins, 2003), 340.

14 Muslim bin al-Ḥajjāj, *Ṣaḥīḥ Muslim*, ʿAbdul Ḥamīd Ṣiddiqī, trans. (Lahore, Pakistan: Sh. Muḥammad Ashraf, 1976), 4:1362, no. 6221; Ibn Mājah, *al-Sunan* (Riyāẓ, Saudi Arabia: Dār al-Salām, 1999), 604, no. 4143.

15 Ernest Gellner, *Nations and Nationalism* (Ithaca, London: Cornell University Press, 1983), 112.

16 Abū Ḥamīd al-Ghazālī, *Iḥyā' ʿUlum al-Dīn*, 3:244.

17 See Shihāb al-Dīn b. Abī ad-Dimashqī-Shāfiʿī, *Kitāb Ādāb al-Qaḍā'*, Muḥammad az-Zuḥaylī, ed. (Beirut: Dār al-Fikr al-Muʿāsir, 1402 AH/1982 CE), 111.

18 *Ṣaḥīḥ Muslim*, 4:1365-1366, no. 6246.

19 Dr. Muḥammad Muhsin Khān, *The Meanings of Ṣaḥīḥ al-Bukhārī* (Chicago, Ill: Kazi Publications, 1979), 7:81-82, no. 116.

20 Ibn Ḥajar al-ʿAsqalānī, *Fatḥ al-Bārī: Sharḥ Ṣaḥīḥ al-Bukhārī* (Riyāẓ: Dār al-Salām; Damascus: Dār al-Fayḥa', 1997), 13:141.

21 Abū Dāwūd as-Sajistānī, *Sunan Abū Dāwūd* (Riyāẓ: Dār al-Salām, 1999), 720, no. 5119.

22 *Ṣaḥīḥ Muslim*, 3:1030, no. 4561

23 This incident is mentioned in the Qur'ān, 3:100-101. The text of this verse reads, "*O Believers! If you obey a party from those previously given the scripture, they will return you to disbelief after your faith. How could you ever revert to disbelief while the Scripture of God is yet being revealed and His Messenger is yet with you. Whoever holds fast to the [Religion of] God will be guided to a straight path.*"

24 See Ibn Manẓūr, *Lisān al-ʿArab* (Beirut: Dār al-Ṣādir, 2000), 3:229.

25 William Pfaff, *The Wrath of Nations: Civilization and the Furies of Nationalism* (New York: Simon and Schuster, 1993), 238.

26 For an excellent and concise account of Ibn Battuta's travels, see, Douglas Bullis, "The Longest Hajj: The Jouneys of Ibn Battuta," *Aramco World,* 51:4 (July/August, 2000), 3-39.

Islām, the Prophet Muḥammad ﷺ, and Blackness

One of the most puzzling phenomena associated with the spread of Islām in the United States is its tremendous attraction to African Americans. Many students of religion and society are baffled by that attraction, as they understand Islām to be a religion which has prejudiced black people, contributed to the disappearance of indigenous African religions, and aided the development of the slave trade, which ravaged Africa from the 16th through the 19th centuries. Advocates of this interpretation of Islām's relationship to black people or people of African descent are becoming increasingly vociferous.[1] At the same time, despite a far higher conversion rate, a significantly greater percentage of African Americans hold an unfavorable view of Islām, as compared to whites.[2] It is therefore imperative that Muslims clarify just why Islām has proved so attractive to Africans, African Americans, and indeed people of all races and ethnicities.

In this article, we will endeavor to show how Islāmic teachings view blackness and describe the attitude of the Prophet Muḥammad ﷺ towards black and African people. We will examine some relevant issues relating to the Arabic language, the personal life of the Prophet Muḥammad ﷺ, and some of the policies he initiated. Hopefully, this article will give insight into some aspects of Islāmic teachings that are rarely presented to the English reader and also help towards understanding the continued appeal of Islām to black and African peoples.

This article is not intended to directly address the issue of slavery, nor the glaring institutional racism that has historically characterized many Islāmic societies. These issues are highly nuanced and extremely complex. In that sense, they can only be dealt with adequately in an article that concentrates exclusively on them. It is our intention to deal with both issues in a subsequent study.

Language

Symbols, values, and signification are integral parts of any language. Collectively, these aspects of language provide the culture that nurtures the systematic formation and conveyance of ideas. The ability to systematically form ideas is a precondition for coherent thought. The ability to systematically convey ideas to others is the basis of our interpersonal associations. Our ideas take the form of and are conveyed by words. Words with positive connotations are conducive to the formation of positive thoughts and associations. Words with negative connotations are conducive to the formation of negative thoughts and associations. It is our contention that the negative connotations associated with blackness in the English language help shape the way we think about race here in America.

The meanings of words are governed by their ability to be exchanged for dissimilar things whose value is to be determined and their ability to be compared with similar things whose value is to be likewise established.[3] In this regard, the negativity associated with the word "black" provides a psychological context for ascribing negative values to other things, including people, who are characterized by "blackness."

To illustrate the negativity associated with blackness in the English language, consider the following meanings of the term "black," taken from the American Heritage Dictionary,

> Evil; sinister; cheerless and depressing; soiled; gloomy; angered; sullen; attended with disaster; calamitous; of or designating a form of humor dealing with the abnormal and grotesque aspects of life and society and evoking a sense of the comedy of human despair and failure; indicating or incurring censure or dishonor.[4]

From these meanings a series of negative phrases are derived. For example: black book, black humor, black list, black market, black mass, blackmail, black magic, black sheep, and black plague.

The negative connotations associated with blackness were part of the process that used names, signs, and stereotypes to reinforce ideas of inferiority and superiority in racial and religious relationships here in America and throughout the colonized world. This process, which many scholars refer to as signification, provided a framework that helped Europeans enforce ideas of superiority. However, in the racially charged environment of 20th century America, it also provided African Americans who entered into Islām a framework for asserting a non-European cultural and religious identity. Brent Turner, drawing from the research of Charles Long,[5] summarizes the role of signification in the history of African American Muslims in the following passage,

> Signification was part of the ambiguous heritage of the Enlightenment. For on the one hand, people of color were categorized, stigmatized, and exploited for the purposes of economic and political hegemonies, but on the other, equalitarianism and the universality of humanity were affirmed by critical Enlightenment thinkers such as Thomas Jefferson and John Locke. The black American community was signified during this period as inferior to the dominant group in America. Since slavery, however, Islām has undercut

> this signification by offering black Americans the chance to signify themselves, giving them new names and new cultural identities.[6]

One of the reasons Islām proved a source of positive signification can be found in its generally positive view of blackness and black people. We can see this if we look at the meanings associated with black and blackness in Arabic lexical sources.

Admittedly, the word for black in Arabic, *Aswad*, has some of the negative connotations found in English. This fact is pointed out by many scholars who take a critical view of Islām's position on racial issues, especially when discussing Islām in Africa. Al-Bāqir al-ʿAfīf Mukhtār writes, for example,

> It has been mentioned that, in its symbolic order, Arabic Islāmic culture standardizes the white color and prejudices the black color. In pre-Islāmic poetry, in the Qur'ān, in classical Islāmic jurisprudence (*fiqh*), and in classical as well as modern literature, the white color symbolizes beauty, innocence, purity, hope, etc., whereas the black color symbolizes the opposite of these concepts.[7]

However, Mukhtār's argument is superficial in that he fails to adequately contextualize the meaning of blackness in Arabic and Islāmic sources, some of which he quotes. He also fails to examine the positive associations, ascriptions, and symbols related to the concept. He cites, by way of illustration, the Qur'ānic verse, *On a day some faces will be whitened, and others blackened...* [3:106-107] Many commentators note that this does not refer to physical whitening for the righteous nor physical blackening for the sinners. The great exegete Abū Suʿūd mentions that the whitening and blackening of the face are allegories for, respectively, the manifestation of great happiness or dejection on the Day of Resurrection.[8] That being the case, even though the "whitening" of the face is identified with a positive referent, great happiness, it is not associated with any racial or ethnic grouping in this world, nor does it have any actual association with a physical color. Therefore, it cannot be viewed as a term that prejudices any human group. In fact, the Prophet Muḥammad ﷺ is related as mentioning that on that day in the life hereafter, the faces of black people will be the "whitest."[9]

If one were to interpret the Qur'ān in a literal fashion, which is necessary if we are to see it prejudicing a particular group, then the negativity associated with the term "black," and hence its prejudicing black people, would be offset by other verses, such as, *On the day when the trumpet will be blown, we will gather the wrongdoers with blue eyes.* [20:102] By interpreting this verse literally, as I have translated it, one could say that it clearly prejudices northern Europeans, the people most commonly found with blue eyes. The exegetes clearly dismiss such an interpretation, pointing out that blue here is an allegory for eyes that have been afflicted with cataracts; they take on a bluish color and lose their capacity for sight. Thus will be the state of the wrongdoers on the Day of Resurrection.[10] Again, the verse is void of any worldly racial or ethnic associations or ascriptions, as cataracts afflict people of all races.

Even if one interprets the word "blackening" literally in the aforementioned verse, there are a large number of very positive, non-prejudicial connotations associated with blackness in the Arabic language. This is an issue Mukhtār and others fail to adequately explore. For example, in most Arabic lexicons, we read that black is simply the opposite of white.[11] Associated meanings include: *Sawād*, literally Blackness, meaning a group of palm, or other trees, so-called because of their lushness; the settled areas around a village or town; a great multitude of people (*as-Sawād al-ᶜAẓam*); and great wealth.[12] The two staples of the desert Arab's diet, dates and water, are referred to as the two black things (*al-Aswadān*).[13] It is interesting to note that whiteness (*Bayāḍ*), in some of the contexts mentioned above, has negative connotations. For example, as opposed to developed, settled areas referred to by blackness (*Sawād*), whiteness (*Bayāḍ*) means deserted, void of life, and a wasteland.[14]

The word *sayyid* is from the same root as black or blackness S-W-D. That word means, depending on the context, Lord, master, honorable, virtuous, generous, forbearing, one who bears the abuse of his people, and leader.[15] In this context, for a person to be called, literally, blacker (*Aswadu*) than someone else would mean he is more majestic.[16] An exhaustive examination of this issue would be quite lengthy.

If we turn to religious symbols, we see that these positive connotations of blackness are also present in the theological worldview cultivated by Islām. For example, the cube-shaped edifice that every Muslim faces during his/her daily prayers (*al-Ka'ba*) is constructed of gray stones. It is honorifically referred to as the House of God (*Bayt Allāh*). It is draped in a black covering (*al-Kiswā*).[17] At that black-cloaked house, the only object we are allowed to kiss, as an act of worship, is a black stone (*al-Ḥajar al-Aswad*). In the Tradition of Gabriel,[18] when he appeared before the Prophet Muḥammad ﷺ and a group of his followers in the form of a man, of all of the features that could have been singled out to highlight his striking beauty, his intensely black hair is mentioned (*Shadīd Sawād ash-Sha'r*). Black hair is celebrated in Arab literature as a sign of beauty and virtue. The black seed (*al-Ḥabba as-Sawdā'*) is considered the most beneficial of all medicines, being described as the cure for everything except death.[19]

The color representing the family of the Prophet Muḥammad ﷺ was black. He wore a black turban,[20] a practice widely followed by those claiming descent from him. It is interesting to note that the standard of the Prophet's polity ﷺ was black while his banner was white.[21] The black standard was the more prominent of the two. The Abbasids, whose revolt was nominally undertaken to establish the political authority of the Prophet's family ﷺ, took the black flag as their standard.

When the Qur'ān mentions several colors in juxtaposition, it in no way conveys any negative connotations for black or blackness. God says, *Have you not seen how God sends water from the sky, We bring forth therewith fruit of diverse colors; and in the mountains are streaks of white and red, of various shades, and [others] intensely black.* [35:27][22] In this verse the beauty and majesty of the lofty mountains are mentioned. Their beauty lies in the rich variation of their colors, and black is one of those beautiful colors. In this verse, black is the only color which is emphatically mentioned (*gharābīb sūd*).

Language and symbols provide the basis for our negotiating and understanding reality. As we have attempted to illustrate, Arabic, the language of the Qur'ān, provides a context for positive associations with blackness. Being free from the stultifying hindrance of overt or subliminal racial prejudicing, the Qur'ānic message can be readily assessed on its merits by anyone. It is the message of the Qur'ān that attracts people of all racial and ethnic backgrounds, along with the loftiness of the Prophetic practice. We will now turn to an examination of that practice.

The Prophetic Practice

We wish to introduce in this section, an examination of the Prophetic practice as it relates to his attitude towards his black companions, with a glimpse at a few Islāmic teachings of relevance for understanding the Islāmic position on race. These teachings, when properly understood, work towards eliminating color-based prejudice and racism. We will limit ourselves to a few representative verses from the Qur'ān and a few Prophetic traditions.

God mentions in the Qur'ān, *O Mankind! Surely we have created you from a single pair, a male and female. We then made you into nations and tribes that you come to know one another [not that you despise one another]. The most noble of you with God is the most pious.* [49:13] This verse emphasizes that the values that are meaningful with God are rooted in the content of a person's character, not in any physical features or distinctions. Dividing humanity into nations and tribes facilitates our knowledge of our respective lineages. However, we are discouraged from thinking that those lineages give any of us an intrinsic advantage over another human being. We are reminded that we are all the descendants of Ādam عليه السلام, who was created from dirt.[23]

Hence, any virtue is based on those characteristics that transcend physical accidents and contingencies. The best is the most pious. As piety lies in mindfulness of God, it is a reinforcement of the message conveyed at the beginning of the fourth chapter of the Qur'ān where God, after mentioning the creation of Humanity from a single pair, reminds us, *God is surely watching over you.* [4:1] Our mindfulness of this fact and our appropriate responses in light of it are what distinguishes us.

It is related that the Prophet ﷺ said, "Whoever would be pleased to be the noblest of people, let him be mindful of God."[24] He also said, "Praise to God who has removed from me the burden and arrogance of pre-Islām. People are of two types: a pious believer who is loved by God, and a wretched profligate who is debased by God." He then recited the above verse [49:13].[25] He also said, "Verily, God does not look at your external forms or your wealth. Rather, he looks at your deeds and your hearts."[26] Here, the two greatest sources of external differentiation in human societies are eliminated: race and economic class. Furthermore, two transcendental qualities, righteous deeds and the state of the heart, are stressed. The implications of these teachings for human society, if internalized, are profound.

Elsewhere in the Qur'ān, God emphasizes that the variation of peoples' colors are among His signs, as He says, *Among His signs is the creation of the heavens and the earth, and the variation of your languages and complexions. Surely in this are signs for knowledgeable people.* [30:22] Many of the exegetes mention that the sign in this variation, whose true extent only God knows, is that it all issues from a single parentage.[27] Hence, if we are pleased that God has blessed us with a beautiful hue, we should see that as a glorification of God, not our particular race.

The gist of this discussion is that God never intended physical differences to be the basis of distinctions and prejudicial attitudes between people. In fact, it is Satan who claimed virtue and distinction based on his physical attributes. He says, when ordered to prostrate himself to Ādam ﷺ, *I am better than him. You created me from fire, while you created him from clay.* [7:12] Satan's stand here is instructive from another point of view. In addition to his arrogance, his racism is clearly displayed. For the clay that Ādam ﷺ was created from, was black in color (*Ḥamaʿin Masnūn*).[28] Any racist, regardless of his religion, should know that he is following the footsteps of Satan in his vile attitudes and practices.

The Prophet ﷺ was the best of God's creation. Hence, his exalted standard of conduct was never the basis for any demeaning attitude or behavior. His attitude towards race and race relations affirms that. This can be illustrated by examining his closest and most beloved companions. Before the practice was forbidden by revelation,[29] the Prophet ﷺ adopted Zayd b. Ḥāritha as his son and appended him to his lineage. He stood at the Ka'ba and proclaimed, after Zayd had given preference to him over his very own father, "Bear witness that Zayd is my son!"[30] Thereafter he was known as Zayd the son of Muḥammad. He was nicknamed the Beloved of the Messenger of God (*Ḥibbu Rasūlillah*), owing to the tremendous love the Prophet ﷺ had for him.

Not only did the Prophet ﷺ love Zayd b. Ḥāritha, he trusted him with the command of many of the expeditionary forces that took the field in the early days of Islām. In fact, Zayd b. Ḥāritha was the most prominent Muslim commander during that time. He led the expeditions to al-Qarada in the Najd,[31] to Banī Sulaym at al-Jamūm,[32] to al-ʿĪs,[33] to at-Taraf,[34] twice to Wādī al-Qurā,[35] to Ḥismā';[36] and he was first in command during the fateful Battle of Mu'tah, where he was martyred leading his force of approximately 3,000 Muslims against a Byzantine force numbering upwards to 200,000 men.[37]

The most significant point of his story, as it relates to this article, is that Zayd b. Ḥāritha is reported to have been black.[38] In *Tanwīr al-Ghabash*, Ibn Jawzi describes him as "a short man, very black, with a flat nose."[39] To the Prophet ﷺ, Zayd was like the son he never had, his own male offspring having all died in their infancy.[40] His color did not affect his love for Zayd in any way.

Baraka bint Tha'laba, who was also known as Umm Ayman, was one of the most beloved people to the Prophet ﷺ. She became his bondswoman after the death of his mother, and he freed her the day that he married Khadīja.[41] She was one of the principal field nurses among the women Companions, attending the Battles of Uhud, Khaybar, and Ḥunayn. The Prophet ﷺ, Abū Bakr, and ʿUmar used to visit her.[42] The Prophet used to refer to her as "My mother after my mother,"[43] and when he looked at her he would say, "This is the last surviving member of my immediate family."[44] She was a black woman of Ethiopian descent.[45]

These two, Zayd b. Ḥāritha and Umm Ayman, married and she bore him a son, Usāma. He was one of the most beloved of all people to the Prophet ﷺ. He was sometimes affectionately referred to as the son of Muḥammad ﷺ.[46] He was also called the beloved of the beloved of the Messenger of God (*Ḥibbu Ḥibbi Rasūlullāh*). Like his mother and father, he was black.[47]

Hence, the lad the Prophet ﷺ adopted and appended to his lineage, the boy he affectionately called his son, and the woman he called his mother, after the death of his biological mother, were all black people. This is the most powerful testimony one can give as to the attitude of the Prophet towards race. Similar affection and honor were afforded to many other black companions.

The prophetic practice regarding race was not confined to his personal life and associations. Rather, in his public policies, he pursued policies which designated the highest offices to some of his black companions. We have mentioned the many commands he entrusted to Zayd b. Ḥāritha. The last force he dispatched before his death was placed under the command of Usāma b. Zayd. Usāma had under his command some of the most eminent Companions, including Abū Bakr and ᶜUmar. He was given that command despite his young age, mentioned variously as being between sixteen to twenty years.

The most esteemed public office in Islām, in terms of its otherworldly reward is the position of the caller to the congregational prayer (*Muᶜadhdhin*). Bilāl was the first and principal holder of this position during the Prophetic period. In fact, the Prophet ﷺ designated the Ethiopians as being especially suited for that office. He said, "The call to prayer is for the Ethiopians..."[48] Bilāl also was the Prophet's ﷺ treasurer. He was referred to by many of the companions as "Our leader." Jābir relates that ᶜUmar used to say, "Abū Bakr was our leader, and he liberated our leader, referring to Bilāl."[49] It is well-known that Bilāl was a black man of Ethiopian lineage.

A policy of deeper implications for Muslim society during the prophetic epoch was his practice of marrying his black companions to the women of aristocratic Arab families. These marriages were intentionally designed to rid his society of prevailing attitudes around class and race-based bigotry. Had this prophetic practice endured, many of the racist attitudes plaguing some contemporary Muslim societies may have been alleviated.

An example of such marriages is that of Zayd b. Ḥāritha, who we have previously mentioned, to Zaynab bint Jaḥsh, before her marriage to the Prophet ﷺ. Zaynab was an exceedingly beautiful and refined Arab woman of noble lineage and exalted character. She was from the Prophet's very family, being the daughter of his paternal aunt, Umaymah. Here she was being called to marry a black man, who had formerly been enslaved. She and her brother resisted the idea of marrying Zayd until the issue was addressed by revelation, *It is not becoming of a believing man or woman, once God and His Messenger have decreed an affair, to have an option to follow their own choice.* [33:36][50] After learning of this verse, Zaynab was pleased and submitted to marry Zayd. Their marriage helped to address both the class and race-based prejudices that were prevalent in Arabian society at that time.

The Prophet ﷺ ordered Zayd's son Usāma to marry Fāṭima bint Qays, another aristocratic Arab woman. Her marriage to Usāma occurred after she was proposed to by both Muʿāwiya and Abū Jaḥm b. Ḥuẓayfa.[51] Both of those companions were of noble Arab lineage. However, the Prophet ﷺ gave preference to Usāma.

Another marriage of this type was that of Julaybīb, a black companion, to the daughter of an Anṣār[52] man whose wife defiantly refused the order of the Prophet ﷺ. However, the daughter, owing to her piety, intervened and asked that the Prophet's decree ﷺ be implemented, expressing her confidence in the wisdom of his decision. The Prophet ﷺ, appreciating her piety, prayed that she be blessed by God and given a life of ease. Their marriage was very successful. Julaybīb was subsequently martyred, slaying seven enemy combatants in his immediate vicinity, before meeting his own demise. The Prophet ﷺ, learning of his state, repeatedly said, "He is of me and I am of him."[53]

These marriages were not isolated events. Hence, one has to see them as part of a conscious policy being undertaken by the Prophet ﷺ to address a flaw in the nascent Muslim polity. I will mention one other marriage of this type. That of a black Arab named Sa'd al-Aswad. Sa'd was of pure Arab lineage, from Bani Sulaym. He came to the Prophet ﷺ and asked him if his dark complexion and unpleasant features would prevent him from entering Paradise. The Prophet ﷺ responded that they would not, as long as he was mindful of his Lord and believed in Him. Sa'd immediately accepted Islām. Sa'd then explained to the Prophet ﷺ that he had searched assiduously for a wife, but had been rejected by all and sundry because of his dark complexion. The Prophet ﷺ sent Sa'd to marry the daughter of ʿAmr bin Wahhāb, a recent convert from Banī Thaqīf, who retained many pre-Islāmic prejudices.

Sa'd went to ʿAmr's door and informed him that the Prophet had ordered him to marry his daughter to him. ʿAmr flatly refused. His daughter, overhearing the conversation between her father and the stranger, interceded telling her father to relent before he was disgraced by revelation. ʿAmr went to the Prophet ﷺ and was strongly rebuked for repulsing Sa'd. ʿAmr promptly married his daughter to Sa'd. As Sa'd was in the market purchasing provisions for his new wife, he heard a caller rallying the faithful for a military campaign. He forgot about his marriage, purchased arms and a steed, and went to the battlefield, where he fought valiantly until he was slain. Learning of his death, the Prophet ﷺ went to him and placed his head in his lap until his grave was prepared. He ordered that his arms and mount be sent to his wife's family, informing them that God had married him to one better than their daughter in Paradise.[54]

Conclusion

There are other aspects of the Prophet's ﷺ public policy that we could examine, such as his twice sending his companions to Ethiopia to live under the protection of an African king, the Negus. However, we will limit ourselves to what we have mentioned above. From these few examples, the prophetic orientation towards race and race relations should be clear. As one can see, Islām, in its foundational teachings, seeks to eradicate the attitudes and prejudices that lead to the emergence of racism and bigotry in society. It is these teachings that have enduring attraction to the legions of people entering Islām from all racial and ethnic backgrounds.

In this country, Muslims have a unique opportunity to contribute towards eliminating the most nagging and festering social ill plaguing our society: race-based prejudice.[55] Unfortunately, many Muslims have endorsed this disease by either refusing to acknowledge its existence, or through their attitudes and actions towards their coreligionists of darker complexions. Both are unacceptable. One of the ways to remove such attitudes is through understanding the imperative given us by our Prophet's teachings ﷺ to work towards the creation of a social order where there is no room for racism. If such work is to be meaningful, it will have to start in our own homes, mosques, and Islāmic centers.

Critics of this article may claim that we have evaded any discussion of the deep institutional racism that has historically plagued the Muslim world and continues to do so. Until that glaring social dysfunction is addressed, they might say a Muslim has no right to criticize racism in American society, a society that has made great strides towards eliminating some of the manifestations of institutional racism from its midst. As we mentioned in the introduction, addressing such issues has not been the purpose of this article.

We might add that as long as the type of institutional racism that leads a disproportionately higher number of African Americans, Hispanics, Native Americans, Native Hawaiians, and other minorities in this country to prisons than to university classrooms, as compared to their white counterparts, there is much work to be done. Similarly, the widespread racist defamation of Arabs, South Asians, and others believed to be from Muslim lands currently occurring in this country indicates that the attitudes and social culture that provide a fertile breeding ground for racism remain strong. As long as that is the case, it is imperative that we work against racism here, the land of our birth. Hopefully, our example, if we are serious, will inspire Muslims in other lands to address the deep racism plaguing their societies.

We have the brilliant prophetic example to guide us in undertaking such work. We also have the inspiring lives and examples of countless American Muslims who have been rescued by Islām from the travails of racism. We have no better spokesperson in this regard than Malcolm X, who wrote from the sacred precincts of Mecca,

> During the past eleven days here in the Muslim world, I have eaten from the same plate, drunk from the same glass, and slept in the same bed (or on the same rug)—while praying to the *same* God—with fellow Muslims, whose eyes were the bluest of blue, whose hair was the blondest of blonds, and whose skins were the whitest of white. And in the *words* and in the *actions* and in the *deeds* of the 'white' Muslims, I felt the same sincerity that I felt among black African Muslims of Nigeria, Sudan, and Ghana.
>
> We were *truly* all the same (brothers)—because their belief in one God had removed the 'white' from their *minds*, the 'white' from their *behavior*, and the 'white' from their *attitude*.
>
> I could see from this, that perhaps if white Americans could accept the Oneness of God, then perhaps, too, they could accept in *reality* the Oneness of Man—and cease to measure, and hinder, and harm others in terms of their 'differences' in color.[56]

Notes

1 This sort of analysis of Islām's relationship with Africans and black people is one of the pillars of the Afro-centric movement. See, for example, Chancellor Williams, *The Destruction of Black Civilization: Great Issues of a Race from 4500 BC - 2000 AD* (Chicago: Third World Press, 1987), chapter 5-10.

2 A poll conducted by the Pew Forum on Religion and Public Life and the Pew Research Center for the People and the Press reveals that 44% of African American respondents held an unfavorable view of Islām, compared to 37% of whites who responded. See Scott Keeter and Burke Olsen, "Views of Islām Remain Sharply Divided." *The Pew Research Center for the People and the Press*, September 9, 2004, <http://people-press.org/commentary/pdf/96.pdf>.

3 Anthony Easthope and Kate McGowan, *A Critical and Cultural Theory Reader* (Buckingham: Open University Press, 1992), 9-10.

4 William Morris, ed., *The American Heritage Dictionary of the English Language* (Boston: Houghton Mifflin Company, 1976), 136.

5 See Charles Long, *Signification, Signs, Symbols, and Images in the Interpretation of Religion* (Philadelphia: Fortress Press, 1986).

6 Brent Turner, *Islam in the African American Experience* (Bloomington: Indiana University Press, 1997), 3.

7 Bāqir al-ʿAfīf Mukhtār, "The Crisis of Identity in Northern Sudan: A Dilemma of Black People with a White Culture," *CODSRIA African Humanities Institute Northwestern University*, <www.gurtong.org/ResourceCenter/articles/education/TheCrisisof IndentityinNorthernSudanPres.doc>, 38.

8 Abū Suʿūd al-ʿImādī, *Irshād al-ʿAql as-Salīm ilā Mazāyā al-Kitāb al-Karīm* (Beirut: Dār al-Kutūb al-ʿIlmiyya 199 AH/1419 CE), 2:15.

9 Imran Hamza Alawiye, *Ibn Jawzi's Apologia on Behalf of the Black People and Their Status in Islam: A Critical Edition and Translation of Kitāb Tanwīr al-Ghabash fī Faḍl's-Sūdān wa'l Ḥabash*, Diss. University of London, 1985, p. 146. The term "whitest" here means "most illuminated."

10 See, for example, ʿAbdullāh b. Aḥmad an-Nasafī, *Madārik at-Tanzīl wa'l Ḥaqāʿiq at-Ta'wīl* (Beirut: Dār al-Ma'rifa, 1421 AH/2000 CE), 702.

11 See Ibn Manẓūr, *Lisān al-ʿArab* (Beirut: Dār aṣ-Ṣādir, 2000), 294; and Abū al-Ḥusayn Aḥmad b. al-Fāris, *Maqāyis al-Lugha* (Beirut: Dār al-Kutūb al-ʿIlmiyya, 1420 AH/1999 CE), 1:576.

12 Ibn Manẓūr, 294-296.

13 Ibn al-Fāris, 1:577.

14 Ibn Manẓūr, 2:190.

15 Ibn Manẓūr, 296.

16 Ibn Manẓūr, 297.

17 The Ka'ba is now always draped in black. This practice dates back to the beginning of the ᶜAbbasid Caliphate. However, before that, it was known to have been draped in cloth of various colors.

18 For the text of the Ḥadīth of Gabriel see Ezzedin Ibrahim and Denys Johnson-Davies, trans. *An-Nawawi's Forty Ḥadīth* (Cambridge: Islamic Texts Society, 2003), 28-33.

19 The text of the tradition in its entirety is, ᶜĀ'isha relates that the Prophet ﷺ said, "Surely this black seed is a cure for every disease except *as-Sām*." [ᶜĀ'isha] said, "What is *as-Sām*?" He said, "Death." See Ibn Ḥajar al-ᶜAsqalānī, *Fatḥ al-Bārī: Sharḥ Ṣaḥīḥ al-Bukhārī* (Damascus: Dār al-Fayḥā', 1418 AH/1997 CE), 10:177, no. 5687.

20 Muḥammad Abū ᶜIsa at-Tirmidhī, *Ash-Shamāᶜil al-Muḥammadiyya* (Ḥalab, Syria: Maktaba Usāma b. Zayd), 46.

21 Imām Abū ᶜAbdullāh Muḥammad b. Yazīd b. Mājah, 408, no. 2818.

22 The term *gharābīb sūd* mentioned in this verse can refer to veins of intensely black hue, as I have translated it, or to separate mountains, themselves intensely black in color.

23 See Al-Qur'ān 3:59. This verse reads, *The similitude of Jesus with God is Ādam. He created him [Ādam] from dirt, then said to him, "Be!" and he was.*

24 Quoted by Imām al-Qurtubī in *Al-Jāmi' li Aḥkām al-Qur'ān* (Beirut: Dār al-Fikr, 1407 AH/1987 CE), 16:345.

25 See Imām Suyūṭī's commentary on this verse in Jalāl'd-Dīn as-Suyūṭī, *Ad-Durr al-Manthūr fī't-Tafsīr bi'l Manthūr* (Beirut: Dār al-Ma'rifa, 1970).

26 Ibn Mājah, 604, no. 4143.

27 See Muḥammad ᶜAli ash-Shawkānī, *Fatḥ al-Qadīr* (Beirut: ᶜĀlam al-Kutūb, nd), 4:219.

28 The exegetes say that the term *Ḥamaᶜin Masnūn* refers to "black clay." See, for example, An-Nasafī, 580.

29 See Al-Qur'ān 33:5

30 This incident is related in brief by Ibn Hishām in his biography of the Prophet ﷺ. See Ibn Hishām, *As-Sīra an-Nabawiyya* (Beirut: Dār al-Fikr, 1415 AH/1994 CE), 1:213. Ibn Athīr relates the incident fully. See Ibn

al-Athīr, *Usd al-Ghāba fī Ma'rifa aṣ-Ṣaḥāba* (Beirut: Dār Ihyā't-Turāth al-ʿArabī), 2:282.

31 Samīra az-Zāyid, *Mukhtaṣar al-Jāmi' fī as-Sīra an-Nabawiyya* (Damascus: Samīra az-Zāyit, 1416 AH/1995 CE), 1:403.

32 Az-Zāyid, 2:87.

33 Az-Zāyid, 2:87-89.

34 Az-Zāyid, 2:89.

35 Az-Zāyid, 2:89-90.

36 Az-Zāyid, 2:127.

37 Az-Zāyid, 2:181-190.

38 Although Zayd was black, he was not an African. He was of pure Arab lineage from the Tribe of Kalb. His lineage is mentioned by Ibn Hishām, 1: 212.

39 Alawiye, 132.

40 Before the birth of Ibrahim to Māriya al-Qubṭiyya in Medina, the Prophet ﷺ had two sons by Khadīja in Mecca: al-Qāsim, and ʿAbdullāh, called aṭ-Ṭāhir. They both died in their infancy. See Az-Zāyid, 1:122.

41 Alawiye, 143.

42 Alawiye, 143.

43 Ibn Ḥajar al-ʿAsqalānī, *al-ʿIṣāba fī Tamyīz aṣ-Ṣaḥāba* (Beirut: Dār Ihyā't-Tarāth al-ʿArabī, 1327 AH/1910 CE), 4:432.

44 Ibn Ḥajar, *al-ʿIsaba*, 4:432.

45 Alawiye, 143.

46 Alawiye, 132. It should be noted here that it is common for Arab grandparents to refer to their grandchildren as their sons and daughters, as opposed to grandson or granddaughter.

47 Ibn Athīr, 1:81.

48 Abū ʿĪsā Muḥammad at-Tirmidhī, *Jāmi' at-Tirmidhī* (Riyāẓ: Dār as-Salām, 1420 AH/1999 CE), 885, no. 3936. The full text of this tradition reads, "Political authority lies with the Quraysh, the judiciary is best executed by the Anṣār, the call to prayer is for the Ethiopians, and the trust is best kept by the people of Azd (the Yemenis).

49 Alawiye, 130.

50 Imām Ṭabarī mentions several narrations which relate this incident, and convey Zaynab's approval to marry Zayd in light of this verse and the Prophet's ﷺ request. See Abū Ja'far Muḥammad b. Jarīr aṭ-Ṭabarī, *Jāmi' al-Bayān fī Ta'wīl al-Qur'ān*, 10:301.

51 Ibn Athīr, 7:230.

52 Anṣār refers to members of the Muslim community of Medina who received and assisted the Prophet ﷺ and his companions who had migrated from Mecca to their city.

53 See Ibn Athīr, 1:348. Also, Alawiye, 138-140. The basis of Julaybīb's story is in Ṣaḥīḥ al-Bukhārī. See Ibn Ḥajar, *Fatḥ al-Bārī*, 9:505-506, no. 5283.

54 For a full account of the story of Sa'd al-Aswad see Ibn Athīr, 2:336-337; and Alawiye, 135-138.

55 Our assessment that racism is the greatest problem plaguing American society is not new. W.E.B. Du Bois wrote over one hundred years ago, based on his experience in America, "...the problem of the Twentieth Century is the problem of the color line." W.E.B. Du Bois, *The Souls of Black Folk* (New York: Bantam Books, 1989), xxxi. Well over a half century later James Baldwin would write the following powerful passage, "If we—and now I mean the relatively conscious whites and blacks, who must, like lovers, insist on, or create, the consciousness of the others -do not falter in our duty now, we may be able, handful that we are, to end the racial nightmare, and achieve our country, and change the history of the world." James Baldwin, *The Fire Next Time* (New York: Dell Publishing Co., 1963), 141. For those who feel these are the ruminations of radical intellectuals, Martin Luther King Jr., a member of the black Christian middle class, concluded, after a career struggling for integration, "Yet the largest portion of white America is still poisoned by racism, which is as native to our soil as pine trees, sagebrush, and buffalo grass." James M. Washington, ed., *A Testament of Hope: The Essential Writings and Speeches of Martin Luther King Jr.* (San Francisco: Harper Collins Publishers, 1986), 316. More recently, Dr. Cornel West writes, "Race is the most explosive issue in American life precisely because it forces us to confront the tragic facts of poverty and paranoia, despair and distrust. In short, a candid examination of *race* matters takes us to the core of the crisis of American democracy. And the degree to which race *matters* in the plight and predicament of fellow citizens is a crucial measure of whether we can keep alive the best of this democratic experiment we call America." See Cornel West, *Race Matters* (New York: Vintage Books, 1993), 155-156.

56 Malcolm X and Alex Haley, *The Autobiography of Malcolm X* (New York: Ballantine Books, 1992), 340-341. The italics are included in the original.

Reflections on Black History Month

Black History Month should be of interest to every Muslim, especially in America. It is estimated that up to 20% of the Africans enslaved in the Americas were Muslim.[1] In some areas, such as the coast of the Carolinas, Georgia, and parts of Virginia, the percentages of Muslims in the slave population may have approached 40%.[2] The fact that the search by a random African American, Alex Haley, for his roots led him to a Muslim village in West Africa is indicative of the widespread Muslim presence among the enslaved population here in the Americas.

At this critical time in the history of our country, it is important for Muslims, whose legitimate existence in this country is being challenged in some quarters, to connect to our American Muslim roots. As Muslims, our story in this country did not begin with the coming of Syrians, Lebanese, Albanians, or Yemenis at the turn of the 20th century or later. It began with the lives of those courageous African Muslim slaves whose blood, sweat, and tears were instrumental in building this country. Their struggle is our struggle, and our struggle should be viewed as a continuation of theirs.

In identifying with those African Muslims, we must not allow ourselves to forget that they were part of a greater community; a community that has evolved to almost fifty million African Americans. The struggle of that community—its pain, perseverance, triumphs, and defeats—cannot be separated from the struggle of its Muslim members. If we as Muslims are moved by the suffering of our coreligionists who were exposed to the dehumanizing cruelties of a vicious system, we should similarly be moved by the plight of their non-Muslim African brothers and sisters who suffered the same injustices.

We must also be moved to work with unwavering conviction to address, within the parameters of our organizational missions, the vestiges of institutional racism that continue to disproportionately affect African Americans and other racial minorities in this country. One statistic alone should be sufficient to alert us to the presence of such racism: 50% of this nation's 2.3 million incarcerated individuals come from her 12% African American population. Similarly discouraging statistics are found in areas ranging from access to higher education (or lack thereof), teen pregnancies, high school dropout rates, youth homicides, and many other "quality of death" indicators.

African American Muslims have a particular responsibility in addressing such racism. In beginning to do so, we can take our lead from our formerly enslaved brothers. Despite their lack of freedom, many of them were never "owned." This fact is strikingly clear in their increasingly widespread biographies. Individuals such as Job Ben Solomon (*Ayyūb bin Sulaymān*), Ibrāhīm ʿAbdur-Raḥmān, and Yarrow Mamout, to name a few, did not allow the ravages of chattel slavery to rob them of their dignity, honor, or their human worth.

As we endeavor to address the imperfections of society, in race relations and other areas, we must do so with dignity, honor, grace, and with free and open minds. Those of us who hail from the historically oppressed minority communities of this land must resist the temptation to allow the triumvirate of rage, a sense of victimization, and vengeance to distort our ability to calmly assess and then pragmatically address the many issues confronting us. When such a distortion occurs, delusional thinking and irrational politics usually result.

One of the greatest delusions potentially challenging us lies in seeing our situation as paralleling that of our brothers and sisters in foreign lands governed by repressive, authoritarian regimes. By viewing our situation as parallel to theirs, we are tempted to view the paradigm of resistance that governs their struggles as valid for our situation. Such an assessment is fallacious for a number of reasons.

First of all, most of the significant "Third World" liberation struggles pitted oppressed majorities against oppressive minorities. In this country, the white majority and significant segments of the nonwhite minorities are not so severely affected by structural violence or institutional racism that they view violent or even aggressive challenges to the status quo as legitimate forms of political expression.

Secondly, alternative means of political expression, available in this country, are unavailable in most "Third World" dictatorships or authoritarian oligarchies. Hence, the mechanisms whereby the Jews, by way of example, once a despised and demeaned minority, were able to favorably situate themselves within the system are not available in the Third World countries. Although some of their advancement was facilitated by their ability to benefit from their "whiteness," most of it is due to hard work and effective planning. Similarly, the progress achieved by African Americans in affirmative action—progress that has been steadily eroded, no doubt—could not have been hoped for by oppressed minorities in many other countries. Whether we view these realities as truly empowering or ultimately co-optive does not negate the fact that they do exist. And as long as they exist, they will be powerful mechanisms to damper the appeal and feasibility of radical challenges to the status quo.

Thirdly, while the feasibility of an aggressive, or even violent challenge to the status quo may be debatable in a small, minority-based, "third world" dictatorship, in a society as large, complex, diverse, and as politically conservative as the United States, such challenges would be used to legitimize severe repressive measures that would serve to render even milder forms of dissent less acceptable. While presented here in hypothetical terms, this is actually a recurrent lesson that American history has taught us.

The history of "third world" revolutionary change is no more encouraging. The Algerian experience is illustrative of the legacy of revolutionary violence in Africa. Frantz Fanon, in the *Wretched of the Earth*, his analysis of the Algerian decolonization struggle, saw decolonizing violence as a cathartic agent that would create a new liberated man. The sad reality created by that violence is documented by Fanon in the last chapter of his work. It led to a litany of mental disorders, which Fanon, a trained psychiatrist, documented all too well, and wrecked lives that the leaders of the nationalist struggle were ill-prepared to repair. Furthermore, thirty years later, the heirs of the nationalist regime that the revolution brought to power would be all too willing participants in a bloodbath that would rival anything the former French colonizers had visited upon the Algerian people.

Archbishop Dom Helder Camara, among others, has pointed out that once a spiral of violence begins, it operates on its own internal logic. Injustice leads to revolt. Revolt induces repression. Repression leads to greater injustices, which in turn encourage more radical forms of revolt. These then induce more severe forms of repression. This spiral continues, unbroken. The challenge for theologians in this age, when the potential destructiveness of war is so great it threatens the very existence of our world, is to devise strategies that can meaningfully enhance our collective well-being by peacefully altering the mechanisms of structural violence and institutionalized racism. Muslim theologians, if we are truly "Heirs of the Prophets," peace and blessings of God upon them, should not shy away from this challenge. However, in attempting to meet it, we must resist the temptation to resuscitate the failed strategies, stale ideas, and outdated methods of an ineffective "Third World" revolution.

On the other hand, we must not allow ourselves to be divorced from the struggles of the less fortunate members of the human family. In a not-too-distant past, when standards of political correctness were more closely associated with the truth and not selfish and narrow political agendas, John Kennedy said, "Those who make peaceful revolution impossible will make violent revolution inevitable." The great theologian Reinhold Niebubr declared, "In the social struggle we are either on the side of privilege or need." If these two white Americans, who were "privileged" in every sense of that somewhat trite expression, can advocate for the need to challenge oppressive social relations, it would be an unforgivable travesty for our voices to fall silent.

The question for us is, "How can we best address the oppressive mechanisms facing us and those facing our coreligionists in so many regions scattered around the globe?" In answering this question, we can gain valuable insight from the lives and struggles of our African Muslim forebears. Superior erudition was the key to the liberation of Job Ben Solomon. Herein is a sign for us. As American Muslims we have been blessed to reside in the most intellectually dynamic society in history. Also, the primal command in our religion is to read. We should enthusiastically pursue the mandate created by these twin facts and push ourselves to become the most educated community on Earth, both in religious and worldly knowledge. In so doing, the miracles that were so clearly manifested in the life of Job Ben Solomon will surely bless our lives. We could then well be the people chosen by God to steward a "miraculous" new era of true social justice.

The dignity, nobility, and erudition of Ibrāhīm ᶜAbdur-Raḥmān, qualities that earned him the epithet "Prince," were instrumental in his liberation from the shackles of bondage. Our day is witnessing the steady degradation of our collective human dignity. We should be a community whose dignity and nobility readily impress all who deal with us and, more importantly, a community whose ethics are a reflection of the true value and depth of the prophetic teachings. Sadly, as Muslims, generally speaking, we have dishonored the prophetic legacy we have been entrusted with. Our ethics oftentimes reflect a utilitarian approach to life. If something proves effective (and effectiveness for many of us is increasingly viewed in terms of money or security), we hasten to find ways to provide it with religious sanction. Such an approach may ensure our short-term prosperity, but it will never open the hearts and minds of masses of people to Islām.

Our forefathers attracted people to Islām and conquered lands with the loftiness of their character and ethics. We oftentimes repulse dignified outsiders who come into our midst. At the height of American chattel slavery, Yarrow Mamout, an elderly Muslim who had gained his freedom, so impressed the artist Charles Wilson Peale with his dignity, nobility, and grace that the latter, who painted six portraits of George Washington, was inspired to paint Mamout. Who among us would inspire a similarly placed artist today?

It is not the purpose of these ruminations to suggest a specific program of empowerment. Power, as the Qur'ān emphatically affirms, is God's to give to whomsoever He chooses.[3] However, a deep knowledge of God, self, and society will certainly yield insights conducive to conformity to the divine ways God has established to invite His empowering grace upon a particular community. Furthermore, history affirms that dignity, nobility of character, and courage have been the indispensable characteristics of those who were able to take the oftentimes unpopular stands that helped to usher in fundamental change, by the Will of God.

In speaking of unpopular stands, we are not merely speaking of those that may place us in opposition to an unjust power structure, but also those that may place us in opposition to our race, tribe, class, or even our coreligionists. Popularity has never been a condition for greatness. However, the acts of a great woman may certainly render her popular to those whose lives are bettered by her acts.

In conclusion, Islām is calling us to be bigger than what the world has made us. If the world has made us members of a "disadvantaged" race, class, ethnicity, or gender, the world wants us to be dehumanized by the rage, sense of victimization, and a quest for vengeance that may ensue from these states. The collective weight of those forces, when unrelieved, can easily lead to a loss of hope. For our African Muslim ancestors enslaved in this land, Islām was always a source of hope, dignity, and for many, as we have mentioned, the key to their freedom. For those who never escaped the shackles of physical bondage, Islām provided the basis for their rising above the dehumanization of the chattel system. In the words of Dr. Sylviane A. Diouf, "The African Muslims may have been, in the Americas, the slaves of Christian masters, but their minds were free. They were the servants of Allāh."[4] Let us resolve to build on their legacy.

Notes

1 See Sylvianne A. Diouf, *Servants of Allah: African Muslims Enslaved in the Americas* (New York, London: New York University Press, 1998), 48.

2 Diouf, 47.

3 Al-Qur'ān 3:26-27.

4 Diouf, 210.

Not Muslim Zionists

As Muslims struggle to achieve control of nation-states whose boundaries were created by the European colonial powers, we must be very careful not to become overwhelmed by the urge to make attaining and maintaining Islāmic statehood the end of our earthly striving. The dangers of doing so are many and merit serious consideration by every Muslim "fundamentalist" who is serious about understanding the ramifications involved in the attainment of political power within the current nation-state system. Among the greatest of these dangers is the risk of sacrificing the ethical imperative of Islām to the power imperative of the modern nation-state. In Islām, rituals and institution are not ends in themselves, they are means to a greater end: salvation.

The ultimate end in Islām is to gain the Pleasure and Mercy of God and to enter Paradise. God says, *Whoever obeys God and His Messenger will be entered into Gardens beneath which rivers flow, to dwell therein forever, that is the Great Triumph.* [4:13] Similarly, *the Pleasure of God is Greater, that is the Great Triumph.* [9:72] He also says, *On that day, if the punishment is warded off from anyone, he has received God's Mercy, that is the Clear Triumph.* [6:16]

The acts of worship in Islām are means of improving the character and conduct of the Muslim to help him/her achieve the "Great Triumph". God says in the Qur'ān concerning the ritual prayer, the greatest act of Islām is worship. *Verily the prayer prevents lewdness and indecency.* [29:45] Abū Hurayrah, may God be pleased with him, relates that the Messenger of God ﷺ was informed of a woman who prayed all night and fasted all day, but she abused her neighbor with her tongue. He said, "There is no good in her, she will be in the Hellfire."[1]

These latter narrations illustrate the ethical imperative that Islām encourages. In this world, the goal of a Muslim is to work towards reforming his/her character and actions. Everything else is a means towards that end; including the attainment of power over a state. When the latter is transformed into an end, it is inevitable that ethical and moral principles will be sacrificed. When such a sacrifice occurs, the state becomes a means to distance its supporters away from the ethical and moral principles that the state should be advancing. To illustrate this point one needs merely to examine the history of Zionism and the impact it had on Judaism, especially Reform Judaism.

Zionism is a nationalist movement rooted primarily in 19th century European social and political realities. Early Zionist thinkers such as Nachman Krochmal and Heinrich Eraetz were deeply influenced by Hegelian philosophy. Other European ideas, such as nationalism, imperialism, and ethnocentricity (ideas popularized by the likes of Hegel, Herder, Ranke, Nietzche, Mazzini, and others) were to find their way into the writings of Zionist thinkers such as Moses Hess, Pinsker, Ahad Haʿam and Herzl.[2] This synthesis of European social philosophy and Jewish national consciousness was to create a powerful Jewish nationalism whose focal point would eventually become the establishment of a Jewish state in Palestine.

Zionism, despite its passionate appeal to Jewish tradition and scriptures, was a novel idea among the vast majority of Jews. Its strongest advocates were secularist, or even atheists. It further appeared a time when Reform Judaism was consolidating its appeal among the newly emancipated Jews of Western Europe and America. The Zionist program, which largely rejected any moral or ethical parameters to guide its efforts towards the creation of a Jewish state, was largely antithetical to Reform Judaism. Having rejected both Jewish nationalism and the idea of a "Judenstaat," or state for the Jews, the appeal of Reform Judaism was largely ethical. In the words of Norton Mesvinsky,

> Reform extended another proposition of Traditional Judaism that Jews had been given a prophetic, universalist mission to bring God's message to all human beings. This message was moral and ethical; it beseeched all people to live according to principles of justice and mercy that would finally result in fulfillment of the Messianic promise of peace, brotherhood and righteousness. Jews according to Reform were a "chosen" people only in the sense of being messengers of God's word but in no way did they constitute a nation.[3]

Many Orthodox Jews also opposed Zionism, although for different reasons. A letter written by Rabbi Joseph Hayyim Sonnenfeld in the aftermath of the first Zionist Conference illustrates that opposition,

> With regard to the Zionists, what shall I say and what am I to speak? There is dismay also in the Holy Land that these evil men who deny the Unique One of the World and His Holy Torah have proclaimed with so much publicity that it is in their power to hasten redemption for the people of Israel and gather the dispersed from the ends of the earth. They have also asserted their view that the distinction between Israel and the nations lies in nationalism, blood and race, and that faith and religion are superfluous... Dr. Herzl comes not from the Lord, but from the side of pollution...[4]

Eventually, this resistance to Zionism was overcome owing to a number of factors. The establishment and expansion of a Jewish state in Palestine—the central theme of the Zionist movement—became the central theme of the Jewish religion. By making the return to Palestine, with all of the brutality involved in that return, the focal point of Judaism, the moral and ethical concerns that had historically characterized that faith were downplayed. The Zionist agenda became the Jewish agenda, and wittingly or unwittingly the excesses of Zionism came to be endorsed by Judaism. The rabid ethnocentrism, cynicism, oppression, ethnic cleansing, deceit, murder and mayhem of the Zionist program, all of which would have been condemned by Reform Judaism in its infancy, now encounter no significant opposition from the mainstream Jewish community. This transformation of Judaism has one major cause: it is in the national interest of Israel.

The point we wish to make is that a similar transformation could easily occur in Islām if we Muslims make the attainment of an "Islāmic" state an end towards which all other "religious" considerations must be sacrificed. The nature of the institution of the nation-state and the international state system dictate that there will be discrepancies between the ethical and moral imperatives of Islām and the dictates involved in pursuing a state's national interest. Propaganda may allow for a concealment of that discrepancy, however, as the history of Zionism shows, even the most sophisticated concealment is unmasked by time and the persistence of truth in manifesting itself.

As Muslims we must make a firm, a priori commitment to the truth, morality and ethics, even if by so doing we undermine our ability to achieve or maintain a "state". Ours is a battle for hearts and minds, not territory. When we win the former battle (and it is the easiest one to fight owing to the moral bankruptcy of many modern institutions and ideas), more mundane goals will be achieved in due course. We have an instructive lesson in the example of the early Muslim armies who rather that usurping the lands of the people they conquered were content to live in their garrison towns separate from the conquered folk. When the moral superiority of Islām was demonstrated to those people by the sterling example of the Muslims, the conquered people and their lands were won over for Islām. The uncritical, ill-conceived, abusive exercise of state power can actually retard the moral victory of Islām, just as it has undermined the moral loftiness of Judaism.

Another feature of Zionism that we must avoid is the tendency of political parties or movements to de-legitimize all other schools of thought once they ascend to power. The ascendancy of the Zionist movement to power in the State of Israel meant the effective death of all other interpretations of Judaism. As mentioned above, the ethical orientation of Reform Judaism was crushed. Perhaps even more tragically, the tolerant spirit of Oriental Judaism, which had allowed for a peaceful coexistence with the majority of the Muslim communities of the Middle East and Africa, was permanently altered. This tragedy is captured in the words of the late Ismāʿīl Fārūqī:

> Zionism has terrorized the Jews of the Arab world in order to get them to emigrate to Palestine to fill the homes vacated by the Palestinians. It has thus uprooted them from their lands and the environment in which they lived and prospered for centuries. Besides this robbery, Zionism has imposed upon the Oriental Jews the mentality and ideology of Europe. Racism and ethnocentrism, nationalism and materialism, individualism and utilitarianism, sexual promiscuity and anarchism, nihilism and existentialism, skepticism in knowledge and religion: this is the legacy of Europe imposed upon the Jews of the Orient in the name of "westernization" or "progress". It has destroyed their faith in God and His law. [5]

This consequence of Zionism was inevitable once the movement came to power because Zionism was equated with the Israeli national interest, and vice versa. Furthermore, the Israeli national interest became equated with the greater good of Judaism. Hence, what was good for Israel was good for Judaism, and that which threatened Israel threatened Judaism. Anti-Zionist interpretations of Judaism have to be discredited and suppressed because they are detrimental to Israel's national interest. Anti-Zionist Jews are described as traitors to the Jewish people. Hence, political differences become religious heresy, and religiously-based dissent becomes political treason!

Muslims endeavoring to implement Islām, a universal religion, within the confines of a nation-state run the risk of falling into a similar form of chauvinism. This is especially true in the sense that the current political arrangement in the Muslim world is an extension of colonization. Therefore, most of the Islāmic struggles are national liberation movements. Additionally, most Islāmic movements endorse a specific methodology or approach—mass education, cadre education, clandestine organization, armed struggle, Muslim social activism, etc.—and each tends to view its approach as the most effective and appropriate for the situation it confronts. These features of Islāmic movements contain the seeds of chauvinism, which if combined with the coercive apparatus of the modern state, could result in a heavy-handed attempt to forcibly stifle other interpretations of Islām.

An example of this chauvinism can be glimpsed from the ascension of the House of Saud to power in Arabia. Since consolidating their control over the state apparatus in Arabia, the Saudis have systematically enforced their version of the Ḥanbalī juridical school or what has come to be referred to in some quarters as "Wahhabism." The Saudis' view of Islām has been effectively raised to the level of a state religion, despite the fact that prior to the creation of the Saudi state the adherents of other juridical schools were quite numerous in Arabia. Today those schools and their followers have scant say in "religious" matters; foreign or domestic.

A more contemporary example of this chauvinism can be found in the Iranian Islāmic experiment. Sunnī groups, which questioned the Islāmicity of aspects of the country's constitution, were stifled. Shiʿī groups that challenged the novel idea of Rule of the Jurisconsult (*Wilāyati Faqīh*) were excluded from the political arena. Muslims belonging to the global Islāmic community, who were supposedly represented by the Islāmic regime in Tehran, were given no voice whatsoever in the formulation of foreign policies, even though those policies in many instances contained serious repercussions for Muslims outside of Iran. Dissenters were condemned in Islāmic terms, sometimes being labeled hypocrites (*munāfiqīn*),[6] corrupters (*fāsiqīn*), enemies of the prophetic family (*Amawī*), etc.

The challenge for Muslims aspiring to control a state is to realize that no one movement can speak for all Muslims. Furthermore, the Islāmic movement in any one country cannot claim to be a reflection or representative of the universal Islāmic community; as long as it organizes itself along nationalist lines and tries to implement its interpretation of Islām through institutions that were created to facilitate secular not Islāmic rule. Those institutions by nature are hierarchical and power-centric. We need a new vision, we need to create new institutions, and we need to learn the lessons being presented to us by contemporary history to ensure that we do not become Muslim Zionists.

Notes

1 This tradition has been declared sound by Al-Ḥākim. It is related by Ibn Ḥibbān, Aḥmad and Al-Bazzār. It is quoted from Adh-Dhahabī, *Kitāb Al-Kabāʿir* (Cairo: Al-Maktabat at-Tawfīqiyya), 160.

2 For an excellent overview of the effect of European intellectual currents on 19th century Zionist thinkers, see Shomo Avineri, *The Making of Modern Zionism* (New York: Basic Books, 1981).

3 Norton Mezvinsky, "Reform Judaism and Zionism", in Roselle Tekiner, et al., *Anti-Zionism: Analytical Reflections* (Brattleboro, Vermont: Amana Books, 1988), 314-315.

4 Rev. Dr. William Walmsley, "The State of Israel: Biblical Prophecy or Biblical Fallacy", in EAFORD and AJAZ, *Judaism or Zionism*, (London: Bath Press, 1986), 49.

5 Al-Fārūqī, "Judaism, Zionism and Islam", in EAFORD and AJAZ, 64.

6 In spite of this criticism, we in no way endorse the terrorist tactics of the Mujahideen Khalq Organization (MKO) who were derisively referred as the Munāfiqīn Khalq by the Iranian government and its supporters.

Trees

TREES

I think that I shall never see
A poem as lovely as a tree.
A tree whose hungry mouth is prest
Against the earth's sweet flowing breast;
A tree that looks at God all day.
And lifts her leafy arms to pray:
A tree that may in summer wear
A nest of robins in her hair:
Upon whose bosom snow has lain:
Who intimately lives with rain.
Poems are made by fools like me.
But only God can make a tree.

In this great American poem, Joyce Kilmer captures the beauty, majesty, and awe to be found in one of God's most intriguing creatures: the tree. One thing that intrigued Kilmer, and possibly all others who would take time to reflect on that marvelous creation, is the tree's constant and intimate communion with God. As he states, "A tree that looks at God all day, and lifts her leafy arms to pray."

Before such a powerfully reverent creation, Kilmer can only sense his own inadequacy and weakness. We humans can produce wonderful, eloquent poetry; but what is a poem that emerges from our frail quills compared to the timeless wisdom and inspiring beauty embodied in a tree, a simple yet infinitely complex creation wrought by the marvelous Hand of God?

Many of us here at Zaytuna have been awed by our own tree, the "Bowing Tree," that aging pine seemingly bowed by the travails of time into a reverent prayer position. That graceful bowing made her shade, her invigorating aroma and, for a legion of youthful climbers, her tempting branches all the more accessible; to be enjoyed and admired by all. Some of the greatest contemporary scholars of Islām have sat beneath her shade. Sacred knowledge has been conveyed under her vigilant watch. And from the safety of the refuge she represented, many have paused to watch as the winter rain gently caressed the green grass unfolding before her.

However, the reverent, bowing tree had not yet completed her life's work. She had a final call to answer. God says in the Qur'ān, *The stars and the trees prostrate [unto Him].* [55:6] Observers of the Bowing Tree over the years noticed that she was inching ever closer to her own prostration. Therefore, it should have come as no surprise when on a fateful, rainy winter night, she completed her devotion, prostrating totally to her Lord. Her majestic head nestled firmly upon the ground, her massive trunk oriented towards the prayer direction, her toes, partially uprooted, curved beneath her. Her life's work done, she is now gone.

Like Kilmer's tree, which highlighted his mortality, and whose majesty served to alert him to the reality of an All-Powerful God, our tree served a similar purpose for many of us. Kilmer would die shortly after penning his poem, gunned down in the killing fields of France during the insanity of the First World War, having barely passed his twenty-second birthday. I am sure that the passing of our tree reminds many of us of our own mortality. There is no permanence in this lower abode. Perhaps it is not coincidental that the very Qur'ānic chapter that mentions the prostration of the trees also reminds us, *All on earth will perish.* [55:26] Reminders of this fact surround us. However, who amongst us will take heed?

Have you not seen how God sets forth a parable?
A good word is like a good tree whose roots are firm
and whose branches reach heaven.
It gives its fruit during every season, by leave of its Lord.
And God sets forth parables to people
that they may be reminded. [14: 24-25]

Flight From the Mosque

In houses that God has permitted to be raised up,
that His Name may be remembered therein.
In them He is glorified, morning and evening. [24:36]

One of the noblest and most beneficial institutions in the history of humanity has been the mosque. It was in the mosque that the great scholars of Islām were shaped: linguists, jurists, theologians, saints, as well as countless devout worshippers. The mosque has produced men and women who have left an indelible mark on the world. It was around the mosque that the great universities, hospitals, observatories, hostels, and the other institutions that became the hallmarks of the great Islāmic civilizing enterprise appeared. The mosque has always been the heart of the Islāmic community, serving as a house of worship, an educational center, a center for the dispensing of valuable social services, a meeting place, and a place of solace and refuge.

Unfortunately, today in America, we find many Muslims who have either left, or were never fully involved in the life of the mosque. There are many reasons for this regrettable situation. The purpose of this article is to examine some of those reasons and to suggest some measures that may prove beneficial in overcoming them.

One of the greatest causes of the flight from the mosque is ignorance. This ignorance begins with a lack of knowledge concerning the very word itself. If asked, how many Muslims would know the definition of the word "masjid," the Arabic equivalent of mosque? This may seem a trivial point. However, the meaning of the word is intrinsically associated with its principal function. If we were all more cognizant of the primary function of the mosque, we would possibly be more careful to avoid some of the questionable practices that commonly occur in them. Many of those practices, as we will seek to explain in this article, are instrumental in the flight from the mosque.

The word "masjid" is a noun that means the place of prostration. This particular noun has also been related as "masjad." Ar-Rāzī mentions in *Mukhtār aṣ-Ṣihāh,*

> Masjad, with an "a" after the "j," is the forehead of the man, in the sense that the trace of his prostration is visible on it."[1]

With respect to Islāmic jurisprudence, masjid means any place of Earth where a Muslim establishes prayer. The proof of this definition is contained in the following prophetic tradition:

> The Earth has been made a place of prayer (*masjid*) for me, and pure. Therefore, any man from my community, who is overtaken by the time of prayer, let him pray [wherever he may be].[2]

This facilitation is among the distinctions given to our community. Qāḍī ʿIyāḍ notes, in this regard:

> The believers before us would only pray in demarcated areas whose purity was ascertained. We have been distinguished by being able to pray anywhere on Earth, except in those areas whose filthiness has been ascertained.[3]

The word masjid has then been conventionally applied to a specific place that has been consecrated to accommodate the five daily prayers. Other places where prayer may occur, such as a prayer room (*Muṣalla*) or a monastery (*Ribāṭ*) or a religious school, are not given the same legal status of the mosque.[4]

Knowing this, we should never lose sight of the fact that the primary function of the mosque is to accommodate prayer and, by extension, other acts of worship. We should strive in our communities to make the mosque appealing to the worshippers, regardless of their organizational affiliations. This involves keeping out all unnecessary distractions, beautifying the mosque to make it a place conducive to spiritual devotion, and keeping it clean to minimize the appearance of foul odors, insects associated with filth, and vermin. All of these latter things, when present, diminish the quality of spiritual reflection in one's devotional acts.

Many people fail to realize how important these points are for converts. Many converts are turned away from the mosques because of the confusion and repulsive physical condition that characterizes many of them. Converts from other religious traditions are leaving houses of worship that are the epitome of cleanliness, order, and serenity. One would be hard pressed to find a church or synagogue with food smudged into the carpets, overflowing trash cans inside the sanctuary, devotional literature piled willy-nilly on the bookshelves, filthy bathrooms, and worship services disturbed by roving bands of unruly, undisciplined children. After encountering such situations in many mosques, many converts simply choose to stay home.

Another reason behind the flight from the mosque is the way mosques have been politicized. Almighty God clearly declares in the Qur'ān, *Surely, the mosques are for Almighty God, therefore call on no one along with God.* [72:18]

This politicizing leads to a sectarianism that tears at the unity of our communities. One of the functions of the mosque is unifying the believers. This unifying function can be gathered from reflecting on the description God gives of *Masjid aḍ-Ḍirār*, a mosque the believers have been commanded to never stand in, *There are those who build a mosque by way of mischief and unbelief, in order to disunite the believers...* [9:107]

One of the linguistic implications of this verse is that an acceptable mosque is one that unifies the believers. That unity is based on a communion fostered by the shared devotion of the believers in the mosque. Conflicting political agendas tear at the very heart of that unity. In many instances, those conflicting agendas become associated with particular mosques. We frequently hear terms such as a Salafī mosque, an Ikhwānī mosque, a Ṣūfī mosque, and other such aberrations. Although the orientations that form the basis of these appellations may have great benefit for their individual adherents, when they become exclusionary appendages affixed to the mosque, they can be extremely alienating. This is one of the factors pushing many people away from the House of God.

This politicizing of the mosques sometimes leads to excessive arguing and disputation. In many cases, heated disputes among the defenders of varying interpretations of Islām repulses many Muslims. This is especially true in the case of converts from Christianity who are initially attracted to Islām because of its clarity and the unity of its theology. Muslims in this category are extremely idealistic. Nothing shatters that idealism like sectarian bickering.

Sectarian disputation also has an extremely adverse effect on young Muslims. Most of our youth who have grown up in this country cannot relate to the schisms that underlie many of our disputes. They see themselves as Muslims, period. They are, in many instances, scorned, ridiculed, and in some cases physically abused for merely being Muslims. As the mere fact of being Muslim has such emotive and evocative implications, further dividing the community into battling factions of Ṣūfīs, Salafīs, Taḥrīris, Ikhwānīs, and others is absurd. When anyone, young or old, finds their religion to be an absurdity, they usually end up voting with their feet, choosing the path that leads straight out of the mosque.

Many so-called "modernist" or "secularized" Muslims are similarly repulsed by the situation found in most of our mosques. Such individuals, who sometimes see the mosque as a bastion of "narrow-minded," "backward" fundamentalists, have acclimated to the bureaucratic, administrative, and managerial processes that define modern Western society and are easily frustrated in their efforts to become involved in the activities and running of the mosque. Excessive arguing, administrative and managerial ineptitude, and uninspiring programs try the patience of many individuals who fall into this category.

Multitudes of Muslim women, here in the West, are working in every conceivable field of endeavor. We find among our Muslim sisters: doctors, lawyers, managers, administrators, professors, teachers, and talented, efficient homemakers. Many of them approach the mosque seeking to use their wealth of talents to enhance the programs and running of that institution. In too many instances they find the doors of involvement slammed in their faces, many times by men who themselves have neither the time nor the expertise to make a meaningful contribution to the efficient running of the mosque. As a result, many of our mosques are "dead" institutions. Confronted with this situation, many of our sisters choose not to involve themselves in the life of the mosque.

Many of our youth are also blocked from any effective involvement in the affairs of the mosque, even if they are highly motivated religiously. They gain the impression that they have to wait for the "uncles" to die before they can have any say in the running of the mosque. As the years turn into decades and the same fossilized leadership remains in place, most of the young Muslims eventually get on with their lives. Unfortunately, the role of the mosque in their lives, if they do remain Islāmically active, is minimal. Others, who may not be as religiously committed, drift away from the mosque because there are no viable classes or programs to stimulate them or keep them interested. Sponsorship of youth activities such as team sports, camping, ping pong, and pool are seen as being beyond the scope of acceptable mosque activities.

Finally, in many areas where the percentage of African American or Hispanic converts is too small to support the creation of a mosque in their respective communities, those Muslims are forced to get involved in the activities of the closest "immigrant" mosques. In those mosques, there is the perception of a subtle racism that prevents converts, especially non-white ones, from being meaningfully involved. In many instances, the failure to even acknowledge the existence of any friction between various racial and ethnic groups only serves to alienate converts all the more, leading in many instances to a slow attrition process that results in their gradual migration from the mosque.

Overcoming the flight from the mosque will require a concerted effort on the part of us all, leaders and laity. Below, we list some practical measures that will allow us to enhance the viability of our mosques and hopefully arrest the flight from them.

1. Education – Community leaders will have to endeavor to create and maintain viable education programs that will help to overcome the general lack of knowledge concerning the role of the mosque and its associated rulings. This process of education is also the responsibility of the laity. Each individual Muslim has to work to enhance his or

her understanding of the centrality of the mosque in the life of the Muslim community and then make a commitment to become involved in the life of this indispensable institution.

2. Avoiding Sectarian Politics – No one disputes the role of politics in Islām. Similarly, Islāmic movements and groups have their part to play in the revival of the global Islāmic community. However, the mosque is neither the place for political organizing and recruiting, nor sectarian pontification. The mosque is the House of God, consecrated for His worship. Every other function is secondary. Our homes, schools, campuses, offices, institutes, and meeting halls provide ample platforms for us to present our particular views concerning politics and society. The political neutrality of the mosque must be maintained. By doing so, perhaps our enhanced communion will put more love between our hearts, and this will go a long ways towards ultimately strengthening the community. It should be noted that what is being condemned here is not the discussion of political issues that are of import to all Muslims, but rather using the mosque as a platform to advance sectarian political agendas.

3. Openness – The mosques are for God. We should consciously work to foster an open atmosphere in the mosque, an atmosphere that is inviting to all: men, women, youth, conservatives, modernists, converts, everyone. If we all commit ourselves to the creation of such an atmosphere, we will bring it about. It is essential to remind ourselves that the collective "we" is weightier than the individual "me" in Islām. On the Day of Judgment when all of the people are concerned with themselves, our Noble Prophet ﷺ will be concerned with the entire community, he will

be crying out, "My community! My community! (*Ummatī! Ummatī!*)."

4. Cleanliness – As the adage goes, "Cleanliness is next to Godliness." Our mosques should be a living embodiment of this saying. If we describe them as the "Houses of God" we should make every effort to keep them clean and to beautify them. It is a shame that many Muslims maintain immaculate residences, but pay scant attention to the cleanliness of the mosque. If our edifices are aesthetically appealing, their innate attractiveness alone will encourage their visitation.

A final point we wish to mention is the need to understand the religious stature of the mosque and the virtue of worship in it. We are all familiar with the fact that the congregational prayer in the mosque is twenty-seven times more virtuous than the prayer prayed at home.[5] A great reward is also promised to those who sit in the mosque between the congregational prayers.[6] Similarly, both the Ramaḍān (*Tarāwīh*) prayers and the prophetic tradition of religious retreat (*ᶜItikāf*) encourage all Muslims, male and female, to involve themselves in the life of the mosque during the blessed month of Ramaḍān. The Noble Prophet ﷺ has reminded us that among the people shaded in God's Throne on the Day of Judgment will be a believer whose heart is attached to the mosque.[7] All of these reminders should help to endear the mosque to us and to encourage us to frequent it regardless of the problems plaguing it.

If we can reflect on these reminders, and take the steps we have outlined in this article and others mentioned elsewhere, perhaps we will be able to arrest the flight from the mosque. If we succeed, we can help ensure that a noble institution reassumes its rightful place as the center of our communal life.

Notes

1 Muḥammad Abū Bakr ar-Rāzī, *Mukhtār aṣ-Ṣiḥāḥ* (Beirut, Lebanon: Maktabatu Lubnān, 1985), 121.

2 Ibn Ḥajar al-ᶜAsqalānī, *Fatḥ al-Bārī,* 1:565, no. 335.

3 Quoted in, Muḥammad b. ᶜAbdullāh az-Zarkashī, *ᶜIlām as-Sājid bi Aḥkām al-Masājid* (Cairo, Egypt: Wizāra al-Awqāf, 1996), 27.

4 Az-Zarkashi, 28.

5 Al-Bukhārī, no.618; Muslim, no. 650.

6 Quoted in Imam Abū Zakariyya an-Nawawī, *Riyāẓ aṣ-Ṣāliḥīn* (Damascus, Syria: Dār al-Ma'mūn li't-Turāth, 1994), 342, no. 1065.

7 An-Nawawī, 155, no. 376.

Peace and Justice in Islām

We are living in a world where there could obviously be more peace. As Muslims, we realize this fact more than most people, as the peace of many of our brothers and sisters in various parts of the globe has been tragically disrupted: Palestine, Chechnya, Afghanistan, Kashmir, and other locales. Similarly, we are living in a world where there could be more justice. We read almost daily of assassinations in various parts of the world where terrorist groups, military forces, or intelligence services, oftentimes in summary fashion, declare victims guilty and then proceed to execute them. Unfortunately, such unprincipled political behavior has become increasingly common in both the foreign and domestic policies of this country, causing untold damage to her image and credibility abroad.

These two issues, peace and justice, are joined in the slogans we hear from many activists, especially here in the United States, "No Justice, No Peace!"[1] This linkage is logical, as justice must be considered one of the indispensable prerequisites of any lasting peace. This article intends to briefly look at the ideas of peace and justice in Islām and explore their deeper significance in the life of a Muslim.

Peace

In the Arabic language, the word peace is derived from the radicals S-L-M. The scholars of language mention four closely related terms that can be derived from this origin: *Salām*, *Salāmah*, *Silm*, and *Salm*. Raghīb al-Isfahānī says in his lexicon of Qur'ānic terms, "*As-Salm* and *as-Salāmah* mean freedom from any external or internal ruination."[2] Based on that, he mentions that true peace will only exist in Paradise, for only there will there be perpetuity with no end, complete satisfaction with no need, perfect honor with no humiliation, and perfect health with no disease. In this regard, God is known as *As-Salām*, because He alone is described as being totally free from any defects or flaws.[3] This understanding of true peace being a reality associated with a transformed world is also understood in both Jewish and Christian theology.[4]

At the level of interstate relations, if we ponder the above definition, we can consider peaceful relations between nations as a condition where violence, a state inevitably involving both internal and external ruination, is absent. In this sense, war can be viewed as an aberrational state. The aberrational nature of war is made clearer if we consider that murder, the ultimate consequence of war, is considered an innovation that destroyed the peace formerly existing among the human family. It is stated in a prophetic tradition, "No soul is killed unjustly, except that the elder son of Ādam عليه السلام (Cain) shares in the stain of the crime. That is because he was the first to innovate murder [in the human family]."[5]

At the individual level, peace can be viewed as an absence of the ruinations of the heart. One free from such ruinations will succeed, God-willing, when he/she meets his/her Lord. Therefore, he/she will enter safely into the Abode of Peace (Dār as-Salām). God says in that regard, *[On] the day no amount of wealth or children will be of any benefit. [The only one benefited] will be one who comes before God with a sound (salīm) heart.* [26:89]

If one reflects on these meanings, it should be clear that the wars that Muslims have been involved in throughout our long history do not nullify the validity of the statement, "Islām is the religion of peace." What is meant by that expression, and God knows best, is that Islām provides a path for the human being to enter Paradise (*Dār as-Salām*), and there he/she will know true peace.

Peace has meanings wider than those mentioned above. One of the loftier objectives of our religion is to introduce into the world an ethos that facilitates the spreading of peace at every level. Our personal relations with our fellow Muslims should begin with the implementation of the Prophetic order "Spread peace between you all."[6] This order is so pressing that the Beloved Prophet ﷺ advised its indiscriminate implementation. He said at the end of a tradition in which he described one of the best forms of Islām, "Extend the greeting of peace, to those you know and those you know not."[7] This is a very weighty matter that calls for our deeper reflection. Its weightiness is illustrated by the fact that it is mentioned as being one of the things that completes our faith. The Prophet ﷺ said in that regard, "You will not enter Paradise until you believe, and you will not believe until you love one another. Shall I indicate to you something that will surely lead to your mutual love? Spread the greeting and spirit of peace between yourselves."[8]

Our relations with our spouses should also be characterized by peace. God admonishes us concerning those relations, *And peace is best.* [4:128] Similarly, in our relations with other nations, God commands us, *If they (the enemy) incline towards peace, then you should similarly incline, and place your trust in God.* [8:61] As mentioned above, peace is the original state that prevailed in relations between individuals and societies. This opinion is based, among other narrations, on the saying of the Prophet ﷺ that Jesus ﵇ "will return the world to a state of peace" (*Yurji' as-Salām*) after his appearance at the end of time.[9]

Justice

Our lexicographers define justice, variously, as "to rule based on that contained in the Book of God and the tradition (*Sunna*) of His Messenger ﷺ and refraining from ruling based on empty opinion." It is also defined as "extending inherent rights [to their possessors] equitably."[10] This latter definition emphasizes the importance of equity as an essential aspect of distributive justice.

The concept of justice is one of the essential pillars in the maintenance of both the natural and social orders. God, be He Exalted, has said, *He has established the scale, therefore, do not transgress in the scale [of justice]. Undertake the measuring with justice and do not cheat concerning the scale.* [55:7-8] Justice, as many of our scholars point out, is one of the underpinnings of the order that has been established by God. This reality is also a foundation of a healthy social order. God says in that regard, *O, You who believe! Be upright for God, witnesses to justice; and do not let your hatred of a people move you to a position where you are unjust. Be just, that is closer to piety. Be mindful of God! Verily God is well-informed concerning all that you do.* [4:135]

This social aspect of justice has been beautifully summarized by Imām al-Qurtubī. He says, discussing the relationship between two words that are usually translated as justice (*al-ᶜAdl*), and distributive justice (*al-Qisṭ*), "Justice is the basis of all human relations and a foundation of Islāmic rule."[11] This saying is illustrative of the meaning conveyed by the saying of God, *Verily, We have sent Our Messengers with clear proofs, and We have revealed unto them the Scripture and the Balance in order that they lead people with Justice...* [57:25]

Imām al-Māwardī has summarized the social implications of distributive justice in the following way:

> One of the things that reforms worldly affairs is the principle of distributive justice. It facilitates amicable relations between peo-

> ple, engenders obedience to the Divine Law, and brings about the prosperity of countries. It is the basis of a thriving economy, strong families, and stable government. Nothing devastates the land nor corrupts the mind as quickly as tyranny. That is because there are no acceptable limits [to regulate tyranny].[12]

For this reason, Ibn Taymiyya sees the responsibilities of Islāmic government emanating from a single verse in the Qur'ān, *God enjoins that you deliver the Trusts to their rightful possessors. And when you rule over [or judge between] people, that you do so with justice...* [4: 58][13] The Noble Prophet ﷺ has said in this context, "Surely the most beloved of people with God and the closest to Him on the Day of Resurrection will be a just leader. And the most hated of people and the furthest removed from Him will be a tyrannical leader."[14]

Clearing himself from even an inadvertent association with oppressive, unjust acts, our beloved Prophet ﷺ is reported to have said,

> You bring your disputes to me for adjudication; perhaps one of you is less eloquent than another, and I rule against the wronged party on the basis of what I have heard. Therefore, if I inadvertently grant one of you something owed to his brother do not take it, for I am granting him something that constitutes a piece of Hellfire.[15]

Our impeccably just Khalifa ʿUmar b. al-Khaṭṭāb uttered the following penetrating words:

> Verily, God sets forth parables for you, and He directs admonition towards you in order that hearts will be quickened. Surely, the hearts are dead until God quickens them. Justice has signs and portents. As for its signs, they are shyness, generosity, humility, and gentleness. As for its portents, they are embodied in mercy. He has [likewise] made for every affair a gate, and He has made that gate accessible by providing a key. The gate of justice is a deep consideration of consequences, and its key is otherworldliness. Consideration of consequences ultimately involves remembering death and

> preparing for it by freely parting from one's wealth. Otherworldliness involves dealing justly with everyone and being satisfied with what suffices. If one is not satisfied with what suffices him, no abundance will every enrich him."[16]

Much of this discussion has focused on distributive justice. However, the Qur'ān also places great emphasis on commutative justice. God commands us, *Do not be moved by partiality to discriminate in meting out divinely legislated punishments.* [24:2] The Prophet Muḥammad ﷺ mentioned that one of the reasons behind the ruination of a nation is a lack of commutative justice.[17] In this context, he mentioned that if his very daughter were to steal, he would not hesitate to punish her to the full extent of the law.[18]

In summary, this brief discussion should make it clear to any Muslim that peace and justice are comprehensive concepts with deep implications and we have to be people committed to peace and justice. We must clearly illustrate to the world that our religion is indeed the religion of peace. However, our striving for peace must never allow us to be unjust, nor should it allow us to passively accept injustices. We must take a stand for justice, as we are ordered in the Qur'ān, *Be you upright supporters of justice...* [4:135] However, that stand must go far beyond slogans, such as the one mentioned at the beginning of this article, and move into the realm of positive action; action inspired by the Qur'ān and the words and deeds of our illustrious Prophet ﷺ.

Notes

1 This slogan has been particularly popularized by the New York-based activist Rev. Al Sharpton and his followers.

2 Rāghib al-Iṣfahānī, *al-Mufradāt fī Gharīb al-Qur'ān* (Beirut: Dār al-Ma'rifa, no date), 239.

3 Al-Iṣfahānī, 239.

4 See The Holy Bible, Isaiah, 9:6-7; and John 14:27.

5 Ibn Ḥajar al-ᶜAsqalānī, *Fatḥ al-Bārī*, 13:369, no. 7321.

6 This Hadith is related by Muslim, Abū Dāwūd, and at-Tirmidhī in their collections. Quoted in an-Nawawī, *Riyaẓ aṣ-Ṣaliḥīn*, 289-290.

7 Ibn Ḥajar al-ᶜAsqalānī, *Fatḥ al-Bārī*, 11: 26-27. The full text of the Prophetic Tradition follows: A man asked the Prophet ﷺ "Which Islām is best?" He replied, "That you provide food, and extend the greeting of peace, to those you know and those you know not."

8 This is the full narration of the Prophetic tradition mentioned in note no.4 above.

9 This meaning is narrated in prophetic traditions that are related by al-Bukhārī, Muslim, and Ibn Mājah. See for example, *Fatḥ al-Bārī*, 6:599-600. The above quote is the version of Ibn Mājah. Al-Bukhārī's version mentions that Jesus ﷺ will "put an end to war."

10 These and other definitions of justice are mentioned in Sāliḥ b. ᶜAbdullāh b. Ḥumayd, *Naḍra an-Naᶜīm fī Makārim Akḥlāq ar-Rasūl al-Karīm* (Jeddah: Dār al-Wasīla, 2000), 7: 2792.

11 Quoted in Ibn Ḥumayd, *Nadr al-Naᶜīm*, 8:3153.

12 Quoted in Ibn Ḥumayd, *Nadr al-Naᶜīm*, 7:2793.

13 See Aḥmad b. Taymiyya, *As-Siyasa Ash-Sharᶜīyya* (Beirut: Dār al-Āfāq al-Jadīda, 1983), 4-5.

14 At-Tirmidhī, no. 1329.

15 Ibn Ḥajar al-ᶜAsqalānī, *Fatḥ al-Bārī*, 5:354.

16 Quoted in Ibn Ḥumayd, *Naḍra an-Naᶜīm*, 7:2811.

17 This concept is mentioned at the beginning of the tradition where a lady from Banī Makhzūm, one of the most aristocratic Arab tribes, stole something and the companions were moved to intervene for a lessening of her punishment. The Noble Prophet ﷺ responded, "O people! Those before you were ruined in that if a noble person among them stole something, they left him alone. On the other hand, if a lower class person stole something, they punished him!" See this nar-

ration in its entirety in Abī Zakariyya Yahya b. Sharaf an-Nawawī, *al-Minhāj: Sharḥ Ṣaḥīḥ Muslim* (Beirut: Dār al-Ma'rifa, 1419 AH/1998 CE), 11:186-187, no. 4386.

18 An-Nawawī, *Al-Minhāj*, 11:186-187, no. 4386.

Jihād Is Not Perpetual Warfare

One of the fundamental ideas underlying the argument of those who advocate a clash of civilizations between Islām and the West[1] is the thesis that Islām is a religion that advocates perpetual warfare. This warfare, in their formulation, is what Muslims know as jihād. In his provocative book *Islam Unveiled*, Robert Spencer unequivocally states:

> The jihād that aims to increase the size of the *Dār al-Islām* at the expense of the *Dār al-Harb* is not a conventional war that begins at a certain point and ends at another. Jihād is a "permanent war" that excludes the idea of peace but authorizes temporary truces related to the political situation (*mudāhanah*).[2]

Other Western writers and ideologues go further by linking the idea of jihād to an effort by Muslims to obtain global domination. For example, Daniel Pipes, writing in the November 2002 edition of *Commentary*, states,

> In pre-modern times, jihād meant mainly one thing among Sunnī Muslims, then as now the Islāmic majority. It meant the legal, compulsory, communal effort to expand the territories ruled by Muslims (*Dār al-Islām*) at the expense of territories ruled by non-Muslims (*Dār al-Ḥarb*). In this prevailing conception, the purpose of jihād is political, not religious. It aims not so much to spread the Islāmic faith as to extend sovereign Muslim power (though the for-

> mer has often followed the latter). The goal is boldly offensive, and its ultimate intent is nothing less than Muslim domination over the entire world.[3]

As the pre-modern world never came totally under the sway of Islām, jihād, in the formulation described by Pipes, meant permanent war. Pipes does not see modernity mitigating this pre-modern tendency in jihād, for he goes on to say,

> In brief, jihād in the raw remains a powerful force in the Muslim world, and this goes far to explain the immense appeal of a figure like Osama bin Laden in the immediate aftermath of September 11, 2001.[4]

It is interesting that Spencer, Pipes, and others, buttress their arguments with formulations and concepts associated with classical Islāmic political theory. However, their understanding presupposes a single, narrow reading of the Islāmic tradition, based on certain ideologically determined parameters that limit their ability to accommodate an alternative reading. For example, the often-cited division of the world into Dār al-Ḥarb and Dār al-Islām fits well with attempts to explain the inevitability of a clash between Islām and the West. However, it does not really give us an idea of the nuances and complexities of those terms, nor the diverse ways in which Muslim thinkers, over an extended period of time, defined and actually applied them.

For example, both Abū Yūsuf and Muḥammad b.[5] al-Ḥasan ash-Shaybānī, the two companions of Imām Abū Ḥanīfa, viewed a land governed by the laws of the nonbelievers as constituting a land of disbelief, even if populated by Muslims.[6] Imām ash-Shāfiʿī viewed a land populated by nonbelievers who are not at war with the Muslims as not constituting Dār al-Ḥarb.[7] Therefore, according to these definitions, most of today's Muslim countries, which are governed by secular law codes, are not Dār al-Islām. Conversely, most of the non-

Muslim nations, which are at peace with the Muslim world, are not Dār al-Ḥarb. Such nuances clearly weigh against the simplistic arguments being advanced by a growing wave of anti-Islāmic polemicists and pundits and their Muslim ideological equivalents.

The purpose of this article is to show that while jihād, in one of its classical formulations, could be interpreted as supporting perpetual warfare, there is another reading that argues against that interpretation. In discussing the textual basis of that alternative reading, I will focus on Qur'ān 9:5[8] because of its centrality in the arguments of those endorsing the perpetual war thesis, both Muslim and non-Muslim, and Qur'ān 9:29[9] because of its implications for Muslim-Christian relations.

I will also argue that with the notable exception of the Umayyad "Jihād State," the latter reading has been more instrumental in shaping the foreign policy of Muslim polities, especially in the modern era. In making this point, I will briefly look at the "Jihād State" and present a thesis that explains its inevitable collapse.

A failure on the part of Western ideologues and policymakers to admit the primacy of this "anti-perpetual war reading" of jihād will lead to tragic misunderstandings. These misunderstandings will only serve to deepen the growing resentment and distrust developing between America and the Muslim world and create a political climate conducive to catastrophic wars that could render the Islāmic heartland an uninhabitable waste and greatly increase the likelihood of attacks against the United States as well as her interests abroad.

The "Jihād State" and its Collapse

In his masterful book, *The End of the Jihād State*[10], Dr. Khalid Blankinship argues that the only polity in the history of Islām to base its foreign policy on unmitigated warfare against the non-believers was the Umayyad dynasty, founded by Muʿāwiyyah b. Abū Sufyān. However, this perpetual warfare policy was unsustainable and eventually led to the collapse of the Umayyad state during the reign of Hishām b. ʿAbd al-Malik. The reasons for that collapse can be summarized as follows:

1. The fiscal basis of the regime, predicated on war booty, collapsed.
2. The non-Muslim armies were able to regroup after initial setbacks and sometimes inflicted devastating losses on the Muslim forces.
3. The morale of the Muslim armies faltered; there were even instances where the Muslims refused to fight.
4. A power vacuum was created in the Syrian-Iraqi heartland of the empire. This led to an alteration of the balance of power between the Umayyads and their internal enemies and to the eventual overthrow of the empire by the Abbasids.[11]

The strategic and economic reasons leading to the collapse of the "Jihād State" are quite consistent with what Yale historian Paul Kennedy describes as occurring during periods of "imperial overstretch." Kennedy says in that regard, "The triumph of any one Great Power in this period, or the collapse of another, has usually been the consequence of lengthy fighting by its armed forces...."[12] He also observes,

> Similarly, the historical record suggests that there is a very clear connection in the long run between an individual Great Power's economic rise and fall and its growth and decline as an important military power (or world empire).[13]

Although Kennedy's study focuses on the modern world, his observations provide at least a clue into the strategic and economic dynamics that were pointing towards the eventual collapse of the Umayyad state. These dynamics were noted by both the political and intellectual successors of the "Jihād State" and led to a reformation of the foreign policy of subsequent Islāmic polities. The conclusion that mandated that reformation was that the "Jihād State" is unsustainable.

This conclusion is born out by the fate of the Ottoman Empire, an expansionist Muslim power that did endure into the modern world. Kennedy comments on the Ottoman decline,

> Yet the Ottoman Turks, too, were to falter, to turn inward, and to lose the chance for world domination... To a certain extent it could be argued that this process was a natural consequence of earlier Turkish successes: the Ottoman army, however well administered, might be able to maintain the lengthy frontiers but could hardly expand further without enormous costs of men and money; and Ottoman imperialism, unlike that of the Spanish, Dutch, and English later, did not bring much in the way of economic benefit. By the second half of the sixteenth century the empire was showing signs of strategic overextension...[14]

In any case, the demise of the "Jihād State" led to a permanent restructuring of Muslim political praxis away from a scheme of permanent warfare against non-Muslims, to one which came, over time, to include protracted truces, formal diplomatic relations, and, in the modern world, membership in the international community of nation-states. More importantly, again, in the modern world, this restructuring of Muslim political praxis has led to the implicit and explicit recognition of the institutions and regimes which collectively work to make peace, not warfare, the dominant reality governing the relations between sovereign states. It should be noted that this emerging praxis sometimes conflicted with the theory of "jihād as perpetual warfare," a theory that remained in many legal and exegetical writings, even though, in the modern world, it is a theory that does not inform the foreign policy of even the most radical Islāmic state.

The Perpetual Warfare Thesis: Textual Foundations

Our claim that there is a reading of jihād that argues against perpetual warfare is not a novel one. Although their views do not represent the mainstream, there were many imminent scholars from the early generations of Muslims who saw jihād as constituting a binding obligatory duty only in defensive circumstances or as a generally non-binding obligation. In both cases, the idea of jihād as an unmitigated struggle for global domination is rejected.

Ibn ʿUmar was known to advance the idea of jihād as a non-binding obligation. When he heard ʿAbdullāh b. ʿAmr b. al-ʿĀs mentioning the five pillars of Islām and then adding jihād as a sixth pillar, he strongly rebuked him.[15] Among the generations of the successors and those following them, ʿAṭā', ʿAmr b. Dinār, Ibn Shibrama, and Sufyān ath-Thawrī were all of the opinion that jihād was voluntary.[16]

Among the scholars of the Malīkī rite, Suḥnūn/Saḥnūn is mentioned as having said, "After the conquest of Mecca, jihād became voluntary."[17] Ibn ʿAbd al-Barr is quoted as saying, "[Jihād] is an obligation when one is in a state of insecurity, while voluntary when one is enjoying security."[18]

Among the proof texts marshaled by those holding these opinions are the following:

1. The conditionality involved in the verse *If they fight you, fight them.*[19]
2. Mention of the idolaters initiating hostilities in the verse *Fight the generality of idolaters as they likewise fight you.* [9:35]

3. The order to fight mentioned in the verse *Fighting is prescribed for you...* [2:216] is not to be taken as a binding obligation, rather as a voluntary act.

None of these proofs are irrefutable. Our point has been to mention that the idea of jihād as both voluntary and non-expansive has existed since the earliest days of Islām.

One of the proofs buttressing the case of those Muslims[20] and non-Muslims who claim that Islām advances a theory of perpetual warfare is Qur'ān 9:5, a verse sometimes referred to as the "Verse of the Sword." This verse is said to abrogate all of the verses advocating restraint, compassion, peaceful preaching, mutual respect, and coexistence between Muslims and non-Muslims. Hence, many Western writers cite this verse to justify a state of permanent war between Muslims and non-Muslims. There are also numerous classical Muslim exegetes who explain the verse in a way that supports this perpetual war thesis.[21] However, a closer examination of this verse reveals that this is not how the vast majority of exegetes have understood it.

In properly understanding the "Verse of the Sword," one must place it in context. This verse is part of a series of verses, located at the beginning of the ninth chapter of the Qur'ān, dealing with the polytheists. The first of these verses begins with the statement *[This is] a declaration of immunity from God and His Messenger to those polytheists with whom you have made pacts.* [9:1] In the subsequent discussion of this declaration, many mitigating conditions that argue against the idea of a perpetual, unrelenting war against non-Muslims, are mentioned.

First of all, many of the classical exegetes explain that these verses do not apply to Jews and Christians. Their discussion of the verses in question center on relations with the polytheists to the exclusion of the "People of the Book." For example, Imām al-Qurtubī (d. 671 AH[22]/ 1272 CE), renowned for his exposition on the legal implications of the Qur'anic text, states, concerning the verse in question, "it is permissible to [understand] that the expression 'polytheists' does not deal with Jews and Christians (*Ahl al-Kitāb*)."[23] This opinion is reinforced by the interpretation of a related prophetic tradition "I've been ordered to fight the people until they testify that there is no deity but God."[24] Imām an-Nawawī mentions in his commentary on this tradition, "Al-Khaṭṭābī says, 'It is well-known that what is intended here are the people of idolatry, not the people of the Book (Jews and Christians).'"[25] Among contemporary exegetes, Dr. Muṣṭafā Bughā says, commenting on the term for people (*nās*) that occurs in this tradition, "They are the worshipers of idols and the polytheists."[26] Imām Abū Ḥanīfa, Imām Aḥmad, and most contemporary scholars are of the opinion that the polytheists who are to be indiscriminately fought were those living in the Arabian Peninsula.[27] According to their opinion, the order is now a dead letter because that area has been free from polytheism since the earliest days of Islām.

Just as we can argue, based on a classical understanding of the "Verse of the Sword," that the people who are to be fought against are not an unrestricted class, there are also considerations governing when the restricted classes can be fought. In the verse preceding the "Verse of the Sword," we read, ... *except those you have convened a treaty with from the polytheists; when they have not breeched any of its conditions, nor supported anyone in aggression against you, complete the terms of the treaty*. [9:4]

Imām al-Qurtubī says concerning this verse, "Even if the terms of the covenant are for more than four months."[28] This condition and others mentioned in the verses following the "Verse of the Sword" lead Abū Bakr b. al-ʿArabī (d. 543 AH/ 1148 CE), the great Mālikī exegete and jurist, to conclude, "It is clear that the intended meaning of the verse is to kill those polytheists who are waging war against you."[29] In other words, fighting them is conditional on their aggression against the Muslim community. This position, the permissibility to fight in order to repulse aggression, is the view of the majority of the Sunnī Muslim legal schools as has been explained in great detail by Dr. Muḥammad Saʿīd Ramaḍān al-Būṭī in his valuable discussion of the rationale for jihād.[30]

Another argument against the indiscriminant application of the "Verse of the Sword" is the view of many classical exegetes and jurists that it is abrogated by the verse, *Then, when you encounter the disbelievers in battle, smite their necks; after you have routed them, bind [the prisoners] tightly. Then set them free or ransom them...*" [47:4] The point to be made here is that if an indiscriminate, unconditional order has been given to kill the non-Muslims, how can one have a choice to free or ransom them?

Imām al-Qurtubī mentions that aḍ-Ḍaḥḥāk, ʿAṭā', and others are of the opinion that verse 47:4 abrogates the "Verse of the Sword." Ath-Thawrī relates from Juwaybir, that aḍ-Ḍaḥḥāk said "[The verse] *Slay the polytheists wherever you find them...* is abrogated by the verse *Then set them free or ransom them...*"[31] Imām aṭ-Ṭabarī (d. 310 AH/ 922 CE), the dean of all classical Qur'anic exegetes, reaches the following conclusion concerning this latter verse, after mentioning the proofs of those who opine that it abrogates or is abrogated by the "Verse of the Sword":

> The correct opinion in this discussion, as far as we are concerned, is that this verse [47:4] is effective; it has not been abrogated. This is because the description of what constitutes an abrogating or an abrogated [verse], which has been mentioned in more than one place in this book of ours, occurs when it is not possible to join the two conflicting rulings advanced by the verses or when there is convincing proof that one of the rulings abrogates the other. [In this case] it isn't farfetched to say that a choice has been given to the Messenger of God and those charged with the affairs of the com-

> munity after Him between liberating, ransoming, or executing [the combatant disbelievers].[32]

Hence, Imām aṭ-Ṭabarī holds that the soundest opinion is to join between the two verses. This opinion serves as the basis for the sort of flexibility and moderation that has governed the policy of the Muslim community towards non-Muslims for much of its history. This attitude is supported by other verses in the Qur'ān, all of which argue against the idea of indiscriminate or perpetual warfare against non-Muslims. Among them, *God does not forbid from being kind and equitable to those nonbelievers who have not made war on your religion nor driven you from your homes. God loves those who are equitable.* [60:8] and *If they [the enemy forces] incline towards peace, then you should so incline, and place your trust in God.* [8:61] and, *Fight in the Way of God those who fight you, but do not initiate hostilities. God loves not the aggressors.* [2:190]

Our discussion to this point has focused on Qur'ān 9:5 because of its centrality in the argument of the advocates of the perpetual war thesis. Here, we wish to discuss some issues which arise from Qur'ān 9:29. This verse is critical for Muslims in determining the parameters of our relationship with Jews and Christians. Unfortunately, this verse has been misunderstood by some Muslims and used to advance a theory of constant warfare between the Muslims and the People of the Book (the Jews and Christians). Sayyid Quṭb, in his commentary on this verse, advocates such warfare.[33] Dr. Sherman Jackson has examined some of the methodological flaws of Quṭb's argument in his valuable article *Jihād in the Modern World.*[34] Jackson raises issues relating to alternative Qur'anic verses that mitigate the harsh tone of Qur'ān 9:29, as well as historical developments that force Muslims to reconsider the prevailing legal implications of the verse. Those developments center on the evolution of an international political regime that has made peace the norm governing international relations. This situation is in opposition to pre-modern times when war prevailed.

Even a superficial reading of Qur'ān 9:29 reveals that it cannot be the basis for a scheme that advocates perpetual war. Such a reading clearly indicates that fighting the People of the Book is conditional on their refusal to pay a nominal tribute (*jizya*) in exchange for protection from the Muslim authorities and exemption from military service. Despite the nominal nature of that tribute, there are those, Muslim and non-Muslim, who seek to use the verse as the basis for a scheme that totally humiliates Jews and Christians living in the Islāmic realm. Such attempts are based on the interpretation of the term *wa hum Ṣāghirūn* as meaning "utterly subdued."[35] However, classical exegetes differed on the meaning of this term. Imām aṭ-Ṭabarī mentions several sayings in that regard, including:

> The legitimate interpreters differ as to the meaning of the word "*aṣ-Ṣighār*," which God uses at this point (*wa hum Ṣāghirūn*). Some of them say that he [the Jew or Christian] pays it [the tribute] standing while the recipient is seated.

Imām aṭ-Ṭabarī also says, "Others say [it means] that they bring it themselves, walking, even if they dislike this." In addition, he mentions, "Some say that its mere payment is humbling."[36] All of these interpretations mentioned by aṭ-Ṭabarī and others[37] belie the idea that the *Jizya* is a tribute designed to "utterly subdue" or totally humiliate Jews and Christians living in the Islāmic realm. Rather, the humility is to be manifested at the time of actually paying the tribute and not in debasing or demeaning treatment afterwards. The accuracy of this conclusion is born out by the fact that the expression *wa hum Ṣāghirūn* is an adverbial clause describing the state of those paying the tribute at the actual instance of payment. For this reason, I have translated the relevant passage in this verse as "until they pay the tribute out of hand, with all due humility."[38]

These exegetical understandings are reflected in the writings of the jurists. For example, the scholars agree that anything that would be deemed offensive to a Muslim is forbidden to bring upon a protected Jew or Christian. Anything that would demean, belittle, or oppress a protected non-Muslim is strictly forbidden.[39] This prohibition emanates from the prophetic tradition "As for one who oppresses a protected non-Muslim or belittles or burdens him above his capability (if he employees him) or takes anything from him against his will, I will be his disputant on the Day of Resurrection."[40] It is even forbidden to address him with such terms as "nonbeliever."[41]

Furthermore, the tribute is not universally applicable. For example, it is not to be paid by women, children, unemployed men, those nursing lengthy illnesses, the terminally ill, the blind, the elderly, or bondsmen. In modern times, jurists are in agreement that the tribute mentioned in Qur'ān 9:29 can be applied nominally as the type of taxes modern states levy against the generality of their citizenry. This is based on the precedent of ʿUmar b. al-Khaṭṭāb in his dealings with Banī Taghlib b. Wa'īl. When that Christian Arab tribe protested against the tribute as demeaning, ʿUmar accepted it from them, nominally, in the same manner the poor due was taken from Muslims.[42]

A full expose on this subject would be quite lengthy as there are many aspects of the issue I have not explored. Before moving to the third part of this article, I wish to examine a final issue as it has direct bearing on the situation currently confronting Muslims. It also presents an Islāmic teaching that mitigates the permanence of warfare in Islām. This issue is associated with one of the foundational Islāmic legal principles: "Harm is to be removed."[43] This principle is based on the prophetic tradition "There is no facilitating or reciprocating harm."[44] One of the implications of this principle is giving preference to warding off harm over securing a benefit. Hence, even though jihād has been legislated for Muslims, in circumstances where its prosecution threatens widespread harm to the

Muslim community, it should be left. Al-Khatīb ash-Shirbīnī states in *Mughnī al-Muḥtāj:*

> If the non-Muslim forces are at least double the Muslim force ... and if we feel that we will be annihilated with no chance of victory, it is incumbent upon us to leave [off war].[45]

The current state of the Muslims clearly indicates that at this critical juncture in our history, we should think deeply about the implications of warfare in light of this jurisprudential principle. The increasing destructiveness of modern military technology and the growing gap between the West and the Muslim world are creating a situation where it is becoming increasingly difficult to achieve any of the objectives that underlie Islāmic law through armed conflict. While Muslim nations may well be able to resist and possibly repulse armed aggression from the West, the price associated with such resistance has to be carefully assessed and alternative strategies of resistance considered. We will return to this issue in the second part of this article.

Implications of the Perpetual War Thesis

The above discussion should make it clear that there is a reading of the Islāmic tradition that argues against the idea of jihād as perpetual, indiscriminate warfare. Attempts to present Islām as the new communism, a system locked in a life and death struggle with the West, while making for good ideology, are fundamentally flawed and could lead to disastrous consequences for both the United States and the Muslim World.

In the aftermath of the Cold War, elements of this country's foreign policy establishment had been searching for an enemy menacing enough to justify a huge and wasteful military budget. Throughout the 1990s, rogue states and international terrorism emerged as the most pressing threats to US global interests. These two threats were eventually epitomized by Taliban-dominated Afghanistan, the ultimate rogue state, and Osama Bin Laden,[46] the ultimate terrorist.

However, neither was considered a systemic threat that could rationalize defense budgets exceeding 300 billion dollars annually. China was the only international actor whose stature could even remotely justify such spending. That being the case, confusion prevailed in the defense establishment with all departments preparing for inevitable budget cuts and restructuring. When Osama Bin Laden was implicated in the attacks on New York and the Pentagon, a powerful incentive was presented to a small group of influential neoconservative ideologues to find an underlying motivation that could explain the inevitable appearance of future Bin Ladens. Hence, the "jihād as perpetual war thesis" arose. A perpetual threat to America would mean perpetual preparedness and perpetually large defense budgets to fight Bush's "war that would last a lifetime."

The Pentagon's *Quadrennial Defense Review Report* that was prepared to describe China as the greatest strategic threat to America's international interests prior to September 11, 2001 was subsequently changed by the administration to present "a scruffy band of terrorists—desperate fanatics who exist in tiny numbers and in many places—[as the] principal enemies [of the United States] for the indeterminate future."[47]

Gabriel Kolko and others dismiss the strategic threat posed to US interests by radical Islāmic groups.[48] The inherent weakness of those groups was illustrated by the ease with which the Saudi and Egyptian regimes were able to repulse the challenges of Bin Laden's *al-Qāʿida* and Ayman aẓ-Ẓawāhirī's *al-Jihād al-Islāmī*, respectively, during the mid-1990s.[49]

Despite the innate weakness of such groups, America can do little to destroy them owing to their diffuse nature. Her military machine has been designed to confront the large, standing, fixed-piece army of the former Soviet Union. What she will probably do is engage in jingoistic campaigns such as the 2001 Afghanistan war and the recent invasion of Iraq. These campaigns, while ostensibly undertaken to confront the evil of "terrorism," advance other aspects of her increasingly ill-advised agenda in the Muslim world and only add to the desperation and suffering of ordinary Muslims.

These campaigns will likely bring immediate military victories but long-term political disasters. They will help to create conditions that will swell the ranks of radical Islāmic groups and engender a deep anti-Americanism throughout the Muslim world, making the realization of American interests in the region, without the use of direct force or increasingly venal and ruthless proxy regimes, virtually impossible. Unable to resist through conventional means, radicals are likely to resort to increasingly irrational terrorist attacks that are nearly impossible to predict or effectively combat.

As the pre-Iraq invasion anti-war movement indicated, the American public doesn't desire such wars. Additionally, the draconian measures being taken by our government in the name of combating terrorism are leading to increasingly bold criticisms of America's post 9-11 strategic posture. Domestically, this trend is illustrated by the increased skepticism greeting the efforts of the Bush Administration to explain the dubious claims it made to justify the invasion of Iraq.

Such wars are also undesirable to ordinary Muslims. As for the extreme elements within Muslim ranks, it is time for them to realize that inflammatory rhetoric, irresponsible terrorism, and delusional visions are no substitute for a realistic, pragmatic strategy of empowerment. Just as radical Islāmic groups had no viable deterrent to American air power in Afghanistan, they possess no credible deterrent to the nuclear warheads that have been turned away from their original targets in the former Soviet Union and redirected towards the major population centers of the Muslim world. In addition, along with conventional devises of unproven destructiveness, such as massive fuel-air explosive ordinances, electromagnetic weapons, particle-beam devices, and stun gases that can temporarily incapacitate the population of entire towns, a new generation of tactical nuclear warheads is being developed for use in battles that will ultimately be fought in the Islāmic heartland.[50]

We have seen the devastating effect of nearly 200 tons of depleted uranium (DU) used on armor piercing projectiles during the 1991 Gulf War.[51] Many areas of the Iraqi ecosystem have been contaminated for generations to come. The effects of the untold tons of DU used in the most recent Iraqi campaign will certainly lead to further human and ecological damage.

Similar environmental damage has been caused by tons of incinerated chemical and biological agents as well as spilled and incinerated crude oil and petrochemical derivatives. Unless the reigning climate of irrational confrontation is reversed, we can realistically anticipate similar ecological disasters and their associated human costs as well the possibility of a direct nuclear attack against the defenseless populations of the Muslim World. Mr. Bush has already threatened such an attack.

Changing the current political climate will require a thorough reassessment of all of its ideological premises. Rejecting the "Islām as permanent warfare" thesis is a big step in the right direction. An additional step would involve a total rethinking of our contemporary security paradigm. The current American policy of violent confrontation, vilification, and isolation will only increase the socioeconomic polarization, environmental destruction, and militarization that will combine to produce further instability and violence in the global system, especially in the Muslim world. Such tactics are part of a failed paradigm as the tragedy of September 11, 2001 has made painfully clear. If America acts with courage, wisdom, and vision, she can begin restructuring the international system in ways that truly enhance our collective security. Her failure to do so could lead to a series of increasingly deadly wars that will have no real winners.[52]

Notes

1 Such a "clash" has been popularized by Sam Huntington in his 1993 essay and subsequent book, *The Clash of Civilizations*. See Samuel Huntington, "The Clash of Civilizations?" *Foreign Affairs*, vol. 72, no. 3 (Summer 1993).

2 Robert Spencer, *Islam Unveiled: Disturbing Questions about the World's Fastest Growing Faith* (San Francisco: Encounter Books, 2002), 145.

3 Daniel Pipes, "Jihād and the Professors," *Commentary*, vol. 114, no. 4 (November 2002), 19.

4 Pipes, 20.

5 "b.": abbreviation for "*bin*" or "*ibn*" which means "son of."

6 Muḥammad Khayr Ḥaykal, *Al-Jihād wa'l-Qitāl fīl-Islām* (Beirut: Dār al-Bayāriq, 1996), 1:662-663.

7 Saʿīd Abū Jayb, *Al-Qāmūs al-Fiqhī* (Damascus, Syria: Dār al-Fikr, 1988), 84.

8 This verse reads, *But when the sacred months have passed, slay the polytheists wherever you find them, take them captive, besiege them, and lie in ambush for them everywhere.*

9 This verse reads, "Fight against those People of the Book [Jews and Christians] who do not believe in God or the Last Day, those who forbid not that which God and His Messenger have forbidden, and those who do not accept the Religion of Truth until they pay the tribute out of hand with all due humility."

10 Khalid Yahya Blankinship, *The End of the Jihad State: The Reign of Hishām b. ʿAbd al-Malik and the Collapse of the Umayyads* (Albany, New York: State University of New York Press, 1994).

11 See Blankinship, 6-9 for a fuller summary of these causes.

12 Paul Kennedy, *The Rise and Fall of the Great Powers* (New York: Random House, 1987), xxii.

13 Kennedy, xxii.

14 Kennedy, 10.

15 Quoted in Ḥaykal, 898.

16 See Abū Zakariyya Muhyiddīn an-Nawawī, *Al-Majmū' Sharḥ al-Muhadhdhab* (Beirut: Dār al-Fikr, nd), 19:268-269.

17 Quoted in Ḥaykal, 893.

18 Ḥaykal, 893.

19 Al-Qur'ān 2:191.

20 In modern times, it is difficult to find many Muslims who advocate the idea that jihād embodies a scheme of indiscriminant, perpetual warfare. An example is Bin Laden's infamous 1998 "fatwa" which advocated the indiscriminate killing of Americans and their allies and not all "infidels." For a translation of the most virulent passages of that document, see Bernard Lewis, "License to Kill: Usama Bin Laden's Declaration of Jihād," *Foreign Affairs* vol. 77, no. 6 (November-December 1998), 14-19. A more textually grounded, though distorted, modern day Muslim interpretation of jihād, an interpretation which moves closer to the idea of permanent war, is that of ᶜAbd as-Salām Faraj found in *Al-Farīda al-Ghāᶜiba*, trans. Johannes J. G. Jansen, *The Neglected Duty: The Creed of Sadat's Assassins and Islamic Resurgence in the Middle East* (New York: Macmillan, 1986). Both Faraj and Bin Laden have been influenced by the writings of Sayyid Quṭb, the Egyptian thinker whose seminal writings on jihād and Muslim/non-Muslim relations have influenced many contemporary Islāmic radicals. Quṭb's radical interpretation of Islāmic doctrine can be found in his exegesis of the Qur'ān, *Fī Ẓilāl al-Qur'ān*, (Cairo, Egypt: Dār ash-Shurūq, 1996). His views on jihād have been most cogently stated in *Maᶜālam fī'ṭ-Ṭarīq*, translated as, *Milestones*, (Delhi, India: Markazi Maktaba Islāmi, 1988). This small treatise sets forth the clearest modern day Muslim statement of the jihād as "perpetual war." Quṭb's writings have exerted a powerful influence on a generation of Islāmic thinkers and activists in the 1970's and 1980's. Their importance, therefore, cannot be minimized. However, with the revival of traditional learning in many Muslim societies, the spread of the same among converts during the 1990's, and the strength of the political, anti-jihād branch of the Salafī movement—the followers of Nāsiriddīn al-Albānī—Quṭb's influence is clearly on the wane among today's Muslim youth, even though a small fringe has been "hyper-radicalized."

21 For a forthright presentation of this idea, see for example, Ibn Juzzayy al-Kalbī, *At-Tanzīl li ᶜUlūm at-Tanzīl* (Beirut, Lebanon: Dār al-Arqam, no date), 1:21-22.

22 AH: "After the *Hijra*." The "*hijra*" is the migration of the Prophet Muḥammad ﷺ from Mecca to Medina which took place in 622 CE (Christian Era); this event marks the beginning of the Islāmic calendar.

23 Al-Qurtubī, 8:72.

24 Versions of this ḥadīth are related by Al-Bukhārī: nos. 1399, 1457, 2946; Muslim: nos. 124 – 128; Abū Dāwūd: nos. 1556, 1557; At-Tirmidhī: no. 2607; and An-Nasāʿī: nos. 2442, 3091-3093.

25 An-Nawawī, *Al-Minhāj,* 1:156.

26 Dr. Muṣṭafā Bughā and Muḥyiddīn Mistū, *Al-Wafī: Fī Sharḥ al-Arbiʿīn an-Nawawiyyah* (Damascus, Syria: Dār al-ʿUlūm al-Insāniyyah, nd), 47.

27 For a summary of the jurists' views as to the lawfulness of unrestricted warfare against the polytheists of the Arabian Peninsula, see Ḥaykal, 1456-1457.

28 Al-Qurtubī, 8:71.

29 Abū Bakr Muḥammad b. al-ʿArabī, *Aḥkām al-Qur'ān* (Beirut, Lebanon: Dār al-Fikr, nd), 3:406.

30 See Muḥammad Saʿīd Ramaḍān al-Būṭī, *Al-Jihād fī'l-Islām* (Beirut, Lebanon: Dār al-Fikr, 1997) for an insightful discussion of the rulings and rationale for warfare in Islām. Unfortunately, no English translation is available to date.

31 Al-Qurtubī, 16:227.

32 Aṭ-Ṭabarī, *Tafsīr aṭ-Ṭabarī* , 11:307.

33 See Quṭb, *Fī Ẓilāl al-Qur'ān*, 3: 1619-1650.

34 See in this regard Sherman A. Jackson, "Jihād in the Modern World," *The Journal of Islamic Law and Culture*, 7:1 (Spring/Summer 2002), 22-24.

35 This translation of the term, "*wa hum Ṣāghirūn*," is found in *The Holy Qur'ān: With English Translation* (Istanbul, Turkey: Ilmi Nesriyat, 1996), 190.

36 Aṭ-Ṭabarī, 6:350.

37 See for example, Ibn al-ʿArabī, 2:479-480.

38 See our translation of the entire verse in note 6 above.

39 For a discussion of this issue, see Ḥaykal, 1467-1470.

40 Abū Dāwūd as-Sajistānī, *Sunan Abū Dāwūd* (Riyāẓ: Dār as-Salām), 447, no. 3052.

41 Ḥaykal, 1469.

42 Abū Bakr al-Bayhaqī, *As-Sunan al-Kubrā* (Beirut, Lebanon: Dār al-Kutub al-ʿIlmiyyah, 1994), 9:315, nos. 18, 645.

43 For a discussion of the meaning, textual foundation, and application of this principle, see ʿAli Aḥmad an-Nadwi, *Al-Qawāʿid al-Fiqhiyya* (Damascus, Syria: Dār al-Qalam, 2000), 287-293.

44 This tradition is included by Imām an-Nawawī in his *al-Arbaʿīn*, see bughā, *Al-Wāfī,* 239.

45 Al-Khaṭīb ash-Shirbīnī, *Mughni al-Muḥtāj* (Beirut, Lebanon: Dār al-Ma'rifa, 1997), 4:226.

46 We have retained the spelling popularized by the western media.

47 Gabriel Kolko, *Another Century of War* (New York, NY: The New Press, 2002), 127.

48 For an insightful, balanced assessment of the threat posed by radical and other Islāmic groups, see John L. Esposito, *The Islamic Threat: Myth or Reality* (New York, Oxford: Oxford University Press, 1992). Especially useful is the final chapter, "'Islamic Fundamentalism' and the West."

49 Attempts to overstate the strategic threat posed by Al-Qāʿida are disingenuous and dangerous. Although the threat of random acts of terrorism against American targets is quite real, that threat existed before September 11, 2001 as illustrated by the embassy bombings in Africa and the attack on the USS Cole. However, as a result of increased American vigilance, such attacks are far less likely today. Clearly, military aggression is no way to combat small group terrorism. One must note that it was military aggression, specifically the 1991 Gulf War, which turned Bin Laden, a former ally, against the United States. Virtually all accounts of Bin Laden's life mention the Gulf War as a critical turning point. For a fairly objective, concise treatment of the evolution of Bin Laden's war against America, see Gilles Kepel, *Jihād: The Trail of Political Islām* (Cambridge, Massachusetts: Belknap/The Harvard University Press, 2002), 313-322.

50 A variant of these stun gases was used by the Russians, with disastrous consequences, to end the siege of a Moscow theater by separatists in 2002.

51 For a thorough, if frightening, expose on the origins and dangers of depleted uranium weapons, including their connection to Gulf War Syndrome, see International Action Center, *Metal of Dishonor, Depleted Uranium: How the Pentagon Radiates Soldiers and Civilians with DU Weapons* (New York, NY: Depleted Uranium Project International Action Center, 1997).

52 For an informed critique of the contemporary global security paradigm and the outlines of an alternative arrangement, see Paul Rogers, *Losing Control: Global Security in the Twenty-first Century* (London: Pluto Press, 2000).

Reflections on the Tsunami

By the testimony of time,
surely humankind is in a state of loss... [103:1-2]

The exegetes mention that the testimony of time, mentioned in this verse, refers to the testimony of each era's extraordinary events; events that indicate the incomparable power of God.[1] In our time we have seen many such events. The recent tsunami that devastated regions in and around the Indian Ocean is only the latest. Only God could have ushered the awesome power unleashed by the earthquake that moved the island of Sumatra 10 feet, yet left it intact. Only God could have ushered the awesome power to send a wave of water, whose depth reached from the surface of the water to the ocean floor, hundreds of miles across the sea at speeds exceeding five hundred miles an hour. Only God could devise an "early warning system" that told numerous species of animals to flee to the safety of high ground; only God.

Yet many, even some professing faith in Islam, having seen such an awesome display of God's power, question His Wisdom. Why must our faith be constantly tested? Why did so many unsuspecting people have to perish? Why were children swept from their mothers' arms? Why was there such widespread and apparently wanton destruction?

Why, once again, are Muslims the majority of those suffering from such calamities? Why?

In many instances, for Muslims, such questions may arise from ignorance of basic religious teachings and an insufficient knowledge of Islamic eschatology. Let us endeavor to answer some of the above questions. Perhaps, by so doing we can see the Wisdom of God as it manifests itself in events such as the recent tsunami.

This world, as God repeatedly informs us in the Qur'ān, is the abode of trials and tribulations. God says, *He has created death and life in order to test which of you is best in deed. He is overwhelmingly mighty, oft-forgiving.* [67:2] He also says, *Surely, we will test you with a measure of fear and hunger, and loss of wealth, lives, and the fruit [of your fields and labor]. Give glad tidings to those who patiently persevere.* [2:155] Similarly, *Do people think that they will be left alone merely saying, 'We believe!' and not be tested?* [29:2] All of these verses emphasize that this world is an abode of tests. The object of life is not to avoid or deny its tests and trials, rather to successfully pass them.

Another verse forthrightly presents a fact alluded to in the previous citations. Namely, the tests in this world will involve what we refer to as good and what we refer to as evil. God says in that regard, *Every soul will experience death, and we will test you with evil and good, as a trial; and unto us you will return.* [21:35] This verse makes it clear that God has never promised us a rose garden in this worldly life. Muslims were never promised that we would win every battle.[2] We were never promised that our Muslim community (*Umma*) would march triumphantly through history, in Hegelian or Darwinian fashion, leaving inferior systems of belief and social organization strewn in our wake. And we were certainly never promised that we, contrary to the view of some Islamic thinkers, especially those influenced by positivist philosophy,[3] would be able through science to conquer the forces of nature that have always hung menacingly over the head of humanity, threatening to forever trap us in the "misery of the human condition."

The great sage Ibn ʿAtā'Allāh as-Sakandarī beautifully captured the reality of this world and what our expectations in it should be when he said:

> Do not find the occurrence of tribulations strange as long as you are in this worldly abode, for it [the world] has only manifested its deserved description, its intrinsic characteristic.[4]

Living in this world will inevitably bring us tests. Those tests are subtle and open, they occur in great and small things. Through these tests, God shows those of us who truly believe and those who are empty claimants.[5]

Many think that tests from God are always signs of His wrath. As Muslims, we believe that the trials afflicting us can be signs of His Love. God's Messenger informed us:

> The magnitude of otherworldly reward is proportionate to the magnitude of worldly tribulation. When God loves a people, He tries them. Whoever is content [with God's Decree] will have divine pleasure. Whoever is displeased [with God's Decree] will have divine wrath.[6]

As the Prophets are the most beloved of humanity with God, it follows that their tribulations should be greater than those of ordinary folks. This is indeed the case. The Prophet ﷺ was asked, "Which group of people are most severely tested?" He replied, "The Prophets, then people according to their spiritual rank. People are tested according to their faith."[7] ʿĀ'isha, God be pleased with her, reported, "I never saw anyone more stricken with pain than the Messenger of God ﷺ."[8]

Just as God has informed us that tests and tribulations are the nature of this world, his Messenger ﷺ has informed us that those tests will include earthquakes and other natural disasters. He said, for example:

> The hour will not come until knowledge is taken away, earthquakes become numerous, time passes quickly, tribulations appear, chaos reigns—that is to say widespread killing—[it will not occur] until wealth becomes abundant among you, to a point where it is superfluous.[9]

This particular tradition aptly describes our times. That being the case, we should view the oftentimes unsettling current events as a fulfillment of what our Prophet ﷺ has foretold. The occurrence of these events should only strengthen our faith, deepen our conviction to avoid participating in the strife that he predicted, and inspire us to work to alleviate the suffering of those immediately affected.

Human suffering is real. However, human perseverance and human dignity are just as real. They allow us to nobly endure the trials of this world. As Muslims we are assisted towards this end by our knowledge that any suffering we experience in this world expiates our sins. Our Prophet ﷺ said, "There is no calamity that afflicts the Muslim except for that which God expiates his sins, even [something as slight] as a thorn that pricks him."[10] He similarly declared, "Nothing afflicts the Muslim, neither fatigue, pain, anxiety, sadness, injury, nor grief, even the pricking of a thorn, except for that which God expiates some of his sins."[11]

These narrations call our attention to the fact that the believer's brief stint in this world is a preparation for eternal life. Our understanding of suffering, justice, the trials of this world, and many other issues integral to any meaningful assessment of the human condition are incomplete and inevitably misleading when they are divorced from consideration of the next, eternal life. If one's view of human life is limited to this world, one might easily be led to view the suffering and travails of this world as manifestations of injustice or cruelty. However, when one relates those hardships to the life hereafter, one must confront the question "How bad can any suffering in this world be if it is opens the door to unimaginable, eternal good in the life hereafter?"

In conclusion, those who drowned in the tsunami are martyrs. Those who were crushed by demolished structures are martyrs. Those who will die of dysentery or cholera will be martyrs. They have all gone on or will go on to the good God had prepared for them. Our Prophet mentioned in that regard:

> The martyrs are five:[12] One who dies during the plague; one who dies of dysentery; one who dies by drowning; one who dies in a demolished structure; and one who dies struggling in the way of God.[13]

Paradise will be theirs. Their cases are closed. As for us, what will be our case? Will we humble ourselves before the awesome power of God, or will we continue to display our destructive hubris? Will we continue to take the blessings of food, clean drinking water, and shelter for granted, or will we fall unto our knees, raising our hands to the sky, our eyes flowing over with tears, thanking God for these blessings from the depth of our hearts? Will we forget about the suffering victims of the tsunami as soon as the gatekeepers decide that other stories are more newsworthy and the images disappear from our televisions, or will we continue our relief and fundraising efforts? And perhaps most importantly, will we watch scores of people bury their dead and continue to neglect preparation for our own inevitable demise?

Notes

1 See, for example, Muḥammad ʿAli Aṣ-Ṣābūnī, *Ṣafwa at-Tafāsir* (Beirut: Dār al-Qur'ān al-Karīm, 1406 AH/1981 CE), 3:600. He says, "He (God), be He exalted, swears by the ʿAṣr, which is the time. It calls attention to what it contains of the age(s) witnessed by humanity, and what it contains of various incredible events, and signs indicating the power of God.

2 One could reflect on the message of Al-Qur'ān 3:140, to ascertain the veracity of this statement. In this verse God mentions, "*These varying fortunes [victory, defeat; strength, weakness; influence, impotence] we alternate between people. This is in order that God shows who truly believes, and that He takes from your ranks martyrs. And God loves not oppressors.*"

3 The influence of Comtean positivism was especially strong in 19th Century Egypt. Its influence on Muḥammad ʿAbduh is undeniable. ʿAbduh wedded that positivism to his effort to create what he viewed as a viable Islamic worldview, along with a viable political and social morality. Abduh then influenced a generation of Islamist thinkers, most importantly Rashīd Riḍā. Through them, positivist thinking became one of the distinguishing features of the 20th Century Islamic movement. For an indication of Comte's influence on ʿAbduh see Albert Hourani, *Arabic Thought in the Liberal Age 1798-1939* (Cambridge: Cambridge University Press, 2003), 138-140.

4 Ibn ʿAtā'Allāh As-Sakandarī, *Al-Ḥikam wa'l Munājā al-Ilāhiyya* (Damascus: al-Maktaba al-ʿArabiyya, nd), 19.

5 Al-Qur'ān 29:3. In this verse, God says, concerning the tests of this world, "*In order that God will show which of you are truthful, and which of you are liars.*"

6 At-Tirmidhī, no. 2396.

7 At-Tirmidhī, no. 2398.

8 At-Tirmidhī, no. 2397. The crushing pain which afflicted the Messenger of God ﷺ occurred during his final illness.

9 Al-Bukhārī, no.1036.

10 Al-Bukhārī, no. 5640.

11 Al-Bukhārī, no. 5641.

12 There are other categories of martyrs. Five are mentioned in this tradition. However, the number here is not meant to be definitive. One may note that even this tradition has been mentioned by al-Bukhārī,

in the *Chapter of Tribulations* (Kitāb al-Fitan), in a section entitled, *Martyrdom Includes Seven Groups In Addition to Those Killed in Battle*. Others mentioned by Ibn Ḥajar in his discussion include: A woman who dies during childbirth; one dying of tuberculosis; one killed defending his wealth, his religion, or his family; one who dies while guarding the frontiers of the Islamic realm; and other categories. See Ibn Ḥajar al-ʿAsqalānī, *Fatḥ al-Bārī,* 6:53-54.

13 Al-Bukhārī, nos. 653, and 2829.

American Muslims, Human Rights, and the Challenge of September 11

The tragic events of September 11, 2001 have called into question many fundamental Islāmic principles, values, and beliefs. The ensuing discourse in many critical areas reveals the weakness of Muslims in making meaningful and substantive clarifications of the Islāmic position on a number of critical issues. The purpose of this paper is to examine one of those issues, human rights, in an effort to identify:

1. How are human rights defined in the Western and Islāmic intellectual traditions?
2. Why are human rights issues of central importance to Islāmic propagation efforts in North America?
3. What are the implications of the tragic events of September 11, 2001 for prevailing Muslim views of human rights?

This paper is not designed to respond to the attacks of those authors who assail the philosophy, conceptualization, formulation, and application of human rights policy among Muslims. Such a response would be quite lengthy and, owing to the complexity of the project, would probably raise as many questions as it resolved. Nor is it an attempt to call attention to the increasingly problematic indifference of the United States government towards respecting the civil liberties and other basic rights of its Muslim and Arab citizens.

We do hope that this paper will help American Muslims identify and better understand some of the relevant issues shaping our thought and action in the critical area of human rights.

Defining Human Rights

A review of the relevant literature reveals a wealth of definitions for human rights. Some of these definitions are quite brief, others more elaborate.[1] However, few of these definitions deviate far from the principles delineated by the Universal Declaration of Human Rights (UDHR), issued by the UN General Assembly in 1948. That landmark document emphasizes, among other things:

> The right to life, liberty, and security of person; the right to freedom of thought, speech, and communication of information and ideas; freedom of assembly and religion; the right to government through free elections; the right to free movement within the state and free exit from it; the right to asylum in another state; the right to nationality; freedom from arbitrary arrest and interference with the privacy of home and family; and the prohibition of slavery and torture.

This declaration was followed by the International Covenant on Economic, Social, and Cultural Rights (ICESCR) in 1966. In the same year, the International Covenant of Civil and Political Rights (ICCPR) was also drafted. These arrangements, collectively known as the International Bill of Human Rights, were reaffirmed in the Helsinki Accords of 1975 and buttressed by the threat of international sanctions against offending nations. When we examine these and other international agreements governing human rights, we find a closely related set of ideas that collectively delineate a system of fundamental or inalienable, universally accepted rights.

These rights are not strictly political, as the UDHR mentions:

> The right to work, to protection against unemployment, and to join trade unions; the right to a standard of living adequate for health and well-being; the right to education; and the right to rest and leisure.

In summary, we can say that human rights are the inalienable social, economic and political rights that accrue to human beings by virtue of their belonging to the human family.

Defining human rights from an Islāmic perspective is a bit more problematic. The reason for this is that there is no exact equivalent for the English term "human rights" in the traditional Islāmic lexicon. The frequently used Arabic term al-Ḥuqūq al-Insāniyya is simply a literal Arabic translation of the modern term. However, our understanding of the modern term, when looked at from the abstracted particulars comprising its definition, gives us insight into what Islām says in this critical area. For example, if we consider the word "right" (*Ḥaqq*), we find an array of concepts in Islām that cover the range of rights mentioned in the UDHR.

If we begin with the right to life, Islām clearly and unequivocally guarantees that right. The Qur'ān states, *Do not unjustly take the life which Allah has sanctified.* [6:151] Similarly, in the context of discussing the consequences of the first murder in human history, *For that reason [Cain murdering Abel], we ordained for the Children of Israel that whoever kills a human being for other than murder or spreading corruption on Earth, it is as if he has killed all of humanity. And whoever saves a life, it is as if he has saved all of humanity.* [5:32]

It should be noted, as the first verse points out, Islām doesn't view humanity as a mere biological advancement of lower life forms. If this were the case, there would be little fundamental distinction between human and animal rights, other than those arising from the advancement and complexity of the human mind. However, Islām views human life as a biological reality that has been sanctified by a special quality that has been instilled into the human being, the spirit (*Rūḥ*).[2] We read in the Qur'ān *He then fashioned him [the human being] and breathed into him of His spirit.* [32:9]

It is interesting to note that this spiritual quality is shared by all human beings and precedes our division into nations, tribes, and religious collectivities. An illustration of this unifying spiritual bond can be gained from considering a brief exchange that occurred between the Prophet Muḥammad ﷺ and a group of his companions. Once a funeral procession passed in front of the Prophet ﷺ and a group of his companions, the Prophet ﷺ reverently stood up. One of his companions mentioned that the deceased was a Jew, to which the Prophet ﷺ responded, "Is he not a human soul?"[3]

Possession of this shared spiritual quality is one of the ways our Creator has ennobled the human being. God says in this regard, *We have truly ennobled the human being...* [17:70] This ennoblement articulates itself in many different ways, all of which serve to highlight the ascendancy of the spiritual and intellectual faculties in man. It provides one of the bases for forbidding anything that would belittle, debase, or demean the human being, and its implications extend far beyond the mere preservation of life.[4] It guarantees his/her rights before birth, by forbidding abortion, except in certain well-defined instances. After death, it guarantees the right of the body to be properly washed, shrouded, and buried. It also forbids the intentional mutilation of a cadaver,[5] even in times of war, and forbids insulting or verbally abusing the dead, even deceased non-Muslims. While these latter points may be deemed trivial to some, they help create a healthy attitude towards all aspects of human life, an attitude that must be present if acknowledged rights are to be actually extended to their possessors.

If we examine other critical areas identified by the UDHR for protection as inalienable rights, we can see that Islām presents a very positive framework for safeguarding those rights. In the controversial area of religious freedom, where Islām is identified by many in the West as a religion that was spread by forced conversion, we find that Islām has never advocated the forced acceptance of the faith. In fact, the Qur'ān unequivocally rejects this idea. *Let there be no compulsion in [accepting] Religion, truth clearly distinguishes itself from error.* [2:256] God further warns His Prophet ﷺ against forced conversions, *If your Lord had willed, everyone on Earth would have believed [in this message]; will you then compel people to accept faith?* [10:99]

In this context, every human being is free to participate in the unrestricted worship of his Lord. As for those who refuse to do so according to the standards established by Islām, they are free to worship as they please. During the Ottoman epoch, this freedom evolved into a sophisticated system of minority rights known as the Millet System. Bernard Lewis comments on that system,

> Surely, the Ottomans did not offer equal rights to their subjects—a meaningless anachronism in the context of that time and place. They did however offer a degree of tolerance without precedence or parallel in Christian Europe. Each community—the Ottoman term was Millet—was allowed the free practice of its religion. More remarkably, they had their own communal organizations, subject to the authority of their own religious chiefs, controlling their own education and social life, and enforcing their own laws, to the extent that they did not conflict with the basic laws of the Empire.[6]

Similarly positive Islāmic positions can be found in the areas of personal liberties, within the parameters provided by the Islāmic legal code. We will return to a brief discussion of those parameters and their implications for an Islāmic human rights regime. However, it isn't the purpose of this paper to engage in an exhaustive treatment of this particular subject.

Stating that, we don't propose that Islāmic formulations in this regard are an exact replica of contemporary Western constitutional guarantees governing human rights policy. Muslims and non-Muslims alike, when examining the issue of human rights within an Islāmic legal or philosophical framework, should realize that human rights regimes, as we know them, are a contemporary political phenomenon that have no ancient parallel. However, we are prepared to defend the thesis that Islām has historically presented a framework for protecting basic human rights, and that it presents a system of jurisprudential principles that allow for the creation of a viable modern human rights regime, totally consistent with the letter and spirit of its teachings.

The Relevance of Human Rights for Islām in America

Islām in America has historically been characterized by a strong advocacy of human rights and social justice issues. This is so because it has been primarily associated with people who would be identified as ethnic minorities. The first significant Muslim population in this country, the enslaved believers of African origin, would certainly fit that description.[7] The various Islāmic movements that arose amongst their descendents appeared in a social and political context characterized by severe oppression. That socio-political context shaped the way Islām was understood by the people embracing it. It was a religion, in all of its variant understandings that was seen as a source of liberation, justice, and redemption.[8]

When the ethnic composition of the Muslim community began to change due to immigration in the 1970s, 1980s, and into the 1990s, the minority composition of the Muslim community remained. These newly arriving non-European immigrant Muslims were generally upwardly mobile. However, their brown and olive complexions, along with their accents and the vestiges of their original cultures served to reinforce the reality of their minority status. This fact, combined with the fact that the most religiously active among them were affiliated with Islāmic movements in the Muslim World, movements whose agenda were dominated by strong human rights and social justice concerns, affected the nature of the Islāmic call in this country, keeping human rights concerns to the fore.

Illustrative of this human rights imperative is the stated mission of the Aḥmadiyya Movement when it began active propagation in America. Muftī Muḥammad Ṣādiq, the first significant Aḥmadī missionary to America, consciously called to a multicultural view of Islām that challenged the entrenched racism prevalent in early 20th century American society.[9] This message presented Islām as a just social force, capable of extending to the racial minorities of this country their full human rights. However, there were strong anti-white overtones of the Aḥmadī message, shaped by Muftī Muḥammad Ṣādiq's personal experience and the widespread persecution of people of Indian descent in America that dampened the broader appeal of the Aḥmadī message. Those overtones were subsequently replaced by the overtly racist proclamations of the Nation of Islām, which declared whites to be devils. In the formulation of the Nation of Islām, Islām came to be viewed as a means for the restoration of the lost preeminence of the "Asiatic" Blackman. This restoration would be effected by a just religion, Islām, which addressed the social, economic, and psychological vestiges of American race-based slavery. In other words, Islām was the agent that would grant the Muslims their long denied human rights.[10]

The pivotal figure who was able to synthesize these various formulations into a tangible, well-defined human rights agenda was Malcolm X.[11] By continuing to emphasize the failure of American society to effectively eliminate the vestiges of slavery, he was an implicit advocate of the justice-driven agenda of the Nation of Islām, even after departing from that movement. His biting criticism of the racist nature of American society—which he often contrasted with the perceived racial harmony of Islām—highlighted by his famous letter from Mecca[12] in which he envisioned Islām as a possible cure for this country's inherent racism, was the continuation of the original multi-cultural message of the Aḥmadiyya Movement. Finally, his evolving thinking on the true nature of the struggle of the African American people and his situating that struggle in the context of the Third World human rights struggle reflected the human rights imperative that figured so prominently in the call of Middle Eastern groups such as Egypt's Muslim Brotherhood and the Indian Subcontinent's Jamaat Islāmi, groups that had a strong influence on the founders of this country's Muslim Students Association (MSA) in 1963.[13]

These various groupings, along with the Dār al-Islām Movement, the Islāmic Party of North America, and Sheikh Tawfīq's Mosque of Islāmic Brotherhood,[14] which would develop in many urban centers during the 1960s and 1970s as the purveyors of an emerging African American Sunnī tradition—a tradition consolidated by the conversion of Malcolm X to the orthodox faith—represented in their various agendas the crystallization of the sort of human rights agenda that Malcolm was hammering out during the last phase of his life. These groups all saw Islām as the key to liberation from the stultifying weight of racial, social, and economic inequality in America.

The Iranian Revolution of 1979 further strengthened this human rights imperative. The revolution was presented by its advocates in America, who were quite influential at the time, as an uprising of the oppressed Muslim masses (*mustaḍʿafīn*) to secure their usurped rights from the Shāh, an oppressive tyrant (*ṭāghūt*). This message, conveyed strongly and forcefully through the call of the Muslim Students Association-Persian Speaking Group (MSA-PSG), was extremely influential in shaping the human rights imperative in American Islām, not only because of its direct influence, but also because of the vernacular of struggle it introduced into the conceptual universe of many American Muslims and the way it shaped the message of contending Sunnī groups. The combined influence of these forces worked to insure that human rights issues were prominent in the call of Islāmic organizations and individuals prior to the tragic events of September 11, 2001.

The Challenge of September 11, 2001

The tragic events of September 11, 2001 present a clear challenge to the human rights/social justice imperative of Muslims in North America. The reasons for this are many and complex. The apocalyptic nature of the attacks of September 11, 2001, particularly the assault on and subsequent collapse of the World Trade Center towers, led many observers to question the humaneness of a religion that could encourage such senseless, barbaric slaughter. Islām, the religion identified as providing the motivation for those horrific attacks, was brought into the public spotlight as being, in the view of many of its harshest critics, an anti-intellectual, nihilistic, violent, chauvinistic atavism.[15]

The atavistic nature of Islām, in their view, leads to its inability to realistically accommodate the basic elements of modern human rights philosophy.[16] This inability was highlighted by the September 11, 2001 attacks in a number of ways. First of all, the massive and indiscriminant slaughter of civilians belied, in the view of many critics, any claims that Islām respects the right to life. If so, how could so many innocent, unsuspecting souls be so wantonly sacrificed? Secondly, "Islām's" refusal to allow for the peaceful existence of even remote populations of "infidels," the faceless dehumanized "other," calls into question its respect for the rights of non-Muslims within its socio-political framework. It also highlights its inability to define that "other" in human terms.

As a link between the accused perpetrators of the attacks, Osama Bin Laden, and the Taliban rulers of Afghanistan was developed by both the United States government and news media, the human rights position of Islām was called into further question. The Taliban, by any standards of assessment, presided over a regime that showed little consideration for the norms governing international human rights. Much evidence exists that implicates the Taliban in violating the basic rights of women, ethnic minorities (non-Pashtun), the Shīʿī religious minority, detainees, artists, and others, using in some instances extremely draconian measures. Many of these violations occurred under the rubric of applying what the regime identified as Islāmic law. The news of Taliban excesses and the shock of the events of September 11, 2001 combined to create tremendous apprehension towards the ability and willingness of Islām to accommodate a meaningful human rights regime.[17]

The political climate existing in America in the aftermath of September 11, 2001 has been exploited by certain elements in American society to call into question any humanitarian tendencies being associated with Islām. For example, in the aftermath of the brutal murder of Daniel Pearle, an act whose implications are as chilling as the attacks of September 11, 2001, Mr. Pearle's bosses at the *Wall Street Journal*, Peter Kann and Paul Steiger, remarked, "His murder is an act of barbarism that makes a mockery of everything that Danny's kidnappers claimed to believe in." Responding to those comments, Leon Wieseltier of the *New Republic*, stated, "The murder of Daniel Pearle did not make a mockery of what his slaughterers believe. It was the perfect expression, the inevitable consequence, of what his slaughterers believe."[18] This and similar indictments of Islām challenge the ability of American Muslims to effectively speak on human rights issues in obvious ways.

If we examine the actual nature American Muslim human rights discourse prior to September 11, 2001, we find that it was based in large part on Muslims contrasting the generalities of the Sharīʿa with the specific shortcomings of American society and history in relevant areas of domestic and international policy and practice.[19] This discourse ignored the positive human rights strictures contained in sections of the American constitution, the Bill of Rights, and the UDHR, to which the United States is a signatory. As in other areas, this inadequate approach produced a false sense of moral superiority among Muslims in America. This sense was shattered by the attacks of September 11, 2001, in that many Americans were suddenly pointing to what they viewed as the inadequacy of Islāmic human rights regimes, their inadequate philosophical basis, and their failure to guarantee basic human rights protection, especially for women, religious, racial, and ethnic minorities living in Muslim lands.

Responding adequately to these charges will require a radical restructuring of current Islāmic human rights discourse and the regimes that discourse informs. The generalities that formerly sufficed in that discourse will have to be replaced by concrete, developed policy prescriptions that stipulate in well-defined, legal terms, how viable human rights protections will be extended to groups identified as systematically suffering from human rights abuses in Muslim realms.

An example of the dangerous and inadequate generalities alluded to above can be glimpsed from a brief examination of the Cairo Declaration on Human Rights in Islām (CDHRI). Article 24 of that document states, "All the rights and freedoms stipulated in this Declaration are subject to the Islāmic Sharīʿa."[20] Such a statement is meaningless, considering the vast corpus of subjectively understood literature that could be identified as comprising the Sharīʿa, unless the relevant rulings and principles of the Sharīʿa are spelled out in exacting detail.

While this paper has consciously avoided mention of those features of Islām that would be antithetical to the Western concept of personal liberty, such as the lack of freedom to choose one's "sexual orientation," there are major civil liberties issues that must be addressed, in clear and unequivocal terms, if Islām's human rights discourse is to have any credence. Hiding behind Islām's cultural or religious specificity to avoid providing answers to difficult questions will not advance a deeper understanding of our faith amongst enlightened circles in the West. While making no claim that there will ever be complete compatibility between Islāmic and western human rights schemes, owing to the separate epistemological bases of each approach, there is room for a deeper and clearer articulation of what Islām says about controversial issues such as homosexuality.

Islām has much to contribute in advancing the theory and application of human rights in the West. In *Islam and Human Rights*, Ann Elizabeth Mayer, whose work has been previously cited,[21] acknowledges that,

> The Islāmic heritage comprises rationalist and humanistic currents and that it is replete with values that complement modern human rights such as concern for human welfare, justice, tolerance, and equalitarianism. These could provide the basis for constructing a viable synthesis of Islāmic principles and international human rights...[23]

Perhaps the greatest challenge before us in this regard is successfully identifying those rationalist and humanitarian "currents" and using them in the creation of a viable Islāmic scheme. Doing this will require, among other things, a bold, but mature assessment of the proper relationship between creed and action in the social and political realms. A serious attempt to engage in a rational application of legal principles to contemporary social and political problems in no way implies adopting the methodology of the *Mu'tazila*, medieval Muslim legal and theological rationalists. Using rationality as the standard to assess the veracity of revelation and using rationality as the basis for discovering meaningful Islāmic solutions to pressing social or political problems, in areas where revelation provides no articulated guidance, constitute two entirely different projects.

That being said, our attempts at solving novel contemporary socio-political problems must be guided by well-defined methodologies rooted in the Islāmic tradition. This will help to ensure that we do not succumb to the tremendous appeal of modern American anthropomorphism, a tendency to define God's religion based on our perceived reality, as opposed to using God's religion to help define that reality. Abandoning a major world religion and the great intellectual tradition it has fostered is not wise. We would be the only losers in such folly.

Methodologies appropriate to the nature and objectives of our religion have been developed by Muslim scholars of jurisprudential principles and other aspects of legal thought. These scholars include the likes of Imām ash-Shāṭībī, author of the insightful work, *al-Muwāfaqāt*,[24] Imām ʿIzz al-Dīn b. ʿAbd al-Salām, author of *Qawāʿid al-Aḥkām*, and many others. These writings are part of a rich heritage of scholarship and thought that allowed Muslims to adequately respond to a succession of civilizational challenges throughout our long history. If we are able to master that rich heritage and use the best of it to address the burning issues of our day, we will be able to meaningfully discuss human rights and the full array of issues that currently vex and perplex ourselves and others.

Notes

1 One such concise definition of human rights is mentioned in Paul E. McGhee, "Human Rights," in *The Social Science Encyclopedia*, ed. Adam and Jessica Kuper (London, New York: Routledge, 1985), 369. He states, "Human rights are the rights and freedoms of all human beings." Cyrus Vance presents a much more elaborate definition in which he envisions human rights encompassing the security of the person, meeting his vital needs, civil and political liberties, and freedom from discrimination. Abridged from Cyrus Vance, "The Human Rights Imperative," *Taking Sides: Clashing Views on Controversial Issues in World Politics*, ed. John T. Rourke (Guilford, CT: The Dushkin Publishing Group, Inc., 1992), 254-255.

2 Islāmic scholars have defined the spirit (*Rūḥ*) in various ways. Perhaps the best translation would be "life-spirit." Its true nature is unknown to any human being, although there has been much speculation as to what exactly it is. It is created before the creation of the bodies, which will house it. Worldly life begins with its entrance into the body, and ends with its extraction from the body.

3 This incident is based on a rigorously authenticated tradition, which has been conveyed by Al-Bukhārī, no. 1312; Muslim, no. 2222; and an-Nasāʿī, no. 1920.

4 A beautiful discussion of the ways the human being has been ennobled by God can be found in Imām Fakr al-Dīn al-Rāzī's commentary of the relevant Qur'ānic verse, 17:70. See, Fakr al-Dīn al-Rāzī, *at-Tafsīr al-Kabīr* (Beirut: Dār Iḥyā' at-Turāth al-ʿArabī, 1997), 7:372-374.

5 This practice is condemned based on a tradition related by Imām Aḥmad, Abū Dāwūd, and Ibn Mājah.

6 Bernard Lewis, *What Went Wrong: Western Impact and Middle Eastern Response* (Oxford, New York: Oxford University Press, 2002), 33-34.

7 For a moving, well-document description of the history, lives, institutions, struggles, and legacy of the Africans enslaved in the America, see, Diouf.

8 See, Robert Dannin, *Black Pilgrimage to Islam* (Oxford, New York: Oxford University Press, 2002). Dannin presents a good summary of the evolution of Islām among African-Americans. His book is especially valuable for its detailed treatment of the evolution of the African-American Sunnī Muslim community. See, also Richard Brent Turner, *Islam in*

the African American Experience (Bloomington: Indiana University Press, 1997).

9 Turner, 121-131.

10 For a detailed introduction to the racist ideology of the Nation of Islām, see, Elijah Muḥammad, *Message to the Black Man* (Chicago: Muḥammad's Temple No. 2, 1965). Especially insightful in this regard is a chapter entitled, "The Devil," 100-122.

11 The theme of human rights figured prominently in the political oratory of Malcolm X during the last two years of his life. At the time of his assassination, he was in final stages of a campaign to charge the United States—in the United Nations—with violating the human rights of the then 20,000,000 African Americans in this country. Many observers feel that campaign, a source of great embarrassment for the United States, may have resulted in his death. His views on this subject are presented, among other places, in a speech entitled, "The Ballot or the Bullet" in George Breitman, ed., *By Any Means Necessary* (New York: Pathfinder Press, 1970), 21-22. See, also, "Interview with Harry Ring Over Station WBAI, January 28, 1965," in *Two Speeches by Malcolm X* (New York: Pathfinder Press, 1965), 28-29.

12 Alex Haley with Malcolm X, *The Autobiography of Malcolm X* (New York: Ballentine Books, 1964) 338-342.

13 The Muslim Students Association (MSA) was formed in 1963 among immigrant Muslims. It would eventually evolve into the Islamic Society of North America (ISNA). Formed in 1982, ISNA is the largest Islāmic organization in North America. See, Dannin, 73; and Turner, 236.

14 For a summary of the inter-group dynamics between the Islāmic Party of North America, Dār al-Islām, and Sheikh Tawfīq's Muslim Islāmic Brotherhood, see Dannin, 65-73.

15 For example, The New Republic's Jonah Goldberg refers to Islām as, "...anti-capitalist, alien, sometimes medieval, and often corrupt theocratic fascism." Jonah Goldberg, "The Goldberg File," *The New Republic*, 1 October 2001.

16 Perhaps the most thorough assessment of Islām and human rights is Ann Elizabeth Mayer, *Islam and Human Rights: Tradition and Politics* (Boulder: Westview Press, 1999). Although simplistically lauded by many critics of Islām as "an understated and powerful repudiation of the notion of 'Islāmic Human Rights,'" Mayer's argument is far more

involved. While identifying many of the problems plaguing contemporary Islāmic human rights regimes, Mayer sees Islām's rich tradition as being capable of producing an effective, modern human rights movement.

17 For an indication of the extent of the reported human rights abuses of the Taliban, see Aḥmad Rashid, *Taliban* (London, New York: I.B. Tauris Publishers, 2000), chapters 4,5,8. Also, see Michael Griffin, *Reaping the Whirlwinds: The Taliban Movement in Afghanistan* (London: Pluto Press, 2001), chapter 12.

18 Leon Wiesiltier, "The Murder of Daniel Pearl," *The New Republic*, 25 February 2002.

19 A widely circulated pamphlet, among Muslims, which illustrates this approach is, Mawlana Abū'l ʿAlā Mawdudi, *Human Rights in Islam* (Leicester, England: Islamic Foundation, 1980).

20 This declaration was submitted to the World Conference on Human Rights, Preparatory Committee, Fourth Session. Geneva, April 19 – May 7, 1993.

21 See note 16.

22 Mayer, 192.

23 Imām Ibrahīm b. Mūsā Abī Ishāq ash-Shāṭībī, *al-Muwāfaqāt* (Beirut: Dār al-Ma'rifa, 1997).

24 ʿIzz al-Dīn ʿAbd al-ʿAzīz b. ʿAbd al-Salām, *Qawāʿid al-Aḥkām* (Damascus: Dār aṭ-Ṭibāʿa, 1996).

The Issue of Female Prayer Leadership

Imām al-Jurjānī mentions that *fitna* is "that which clarifies the state of a person, be that good or evil."[1] It is also defined as "strife breaking out among various peoples."[2] In both of these meanings, the controversy surrounding the "historic" female-led Friday (*Jumuʿah*) prayer is a *fitna* for many Muslims in this country. This is undeniable when we see the deep divisions, bitter contestation, and outright enmity it is creating in the ranks of the believers. This is so when we see some people's very faith shaken. This is so when we see spiteful accusations hurled by some Muslims at others. This is so when we see non-Muslims possessed of ill-intent seeking to exploit this controversy to create confusion among the general public and the Muslims as to what Islam is and who are its authoritative voices.

As I consider this controversy a *fitna*, the first thing I wish to say about this matter is that we should all stop for a moment and take time to ask God to protect us. We should ask God that He protects the Muslim community of this land. We should ask that He bless us to have wisdom equal to the challenges He has placed before us. We should ask Him that He grants us all the strength to continue working for Islam in our various capacities. We should ask that He helps us resist the many and increasingly sophisticated efforts to divide us.

After saying that, I wish to clarify my position on this matter. What I write below is based on the Sunnī legal and linguistic tradition, as it has been historically understood. This is the tradition of the Islamic orthodoxy, which remains until today the only religious orthodoxy that has not been marginalized to the fringes of the faith community it represents. My comments will be structured around specific evidences mentioned by Nevin Reda, in an article entitled, "What Would the Prophet Do? The Islamic Basis for Female-Led Prayer."[3]

Of the evidences ushered by Reda in her argument, only one is substantive. Another is ancillary. The rest are considerations that would affect how rulings relating to gender issues might be implemented. However, they have no real weight in establishing a particular ruling in the divine law.

The Tradition of Umm Waraqa

As for her lone substantive evidence, it is the following,

> The Prophet ﷺ commanded Umm Waraqa, a woman who had collected the Qur'ān, to lead the people of her area in prayer. She had her own *muᶜadhdhin* (person who performs the call to prayers).[4]

This narration, found in the compilations of Abū Dāwūd,[5] ad-Dāraquṭnī,[6] al-Bayhaqī,[7] al-Ḥākim,[8] the Ṭabaqāt of Ibn Sa'd,[9] and other sources, is questioned by some scholars of prophetic tradition (*ḥadīth*) because of two narrators in its chain of transmission.[10] The first is al-Walīd b. ᶜAbdullāh b. Jumay'.[11] Imām aẓ-Ẓahabī mentions in *al-Mīzān* that although Ibn Maᶜīn, Imām Aḥmad, and Abū Hātim considered him an acceptable narrator, others refused to accept his transmissions, among them Ibn Hibbān. Imām al-Ḥākim also questioned his probity.[12] Ibn Ḥajar al-ᶜAsqalānī mentions that al-ᶜAqīlī said there was inconsistency in his transmissions.[13]

Although a case can be made for accepting the transmissions of al-Walīd, based on those who do affirm his probity, the state of another narrator in the chain of this tradition, ᶜAbd ar-Raḥmān b. Khallād, is unknown (*Majhūl al-Ḥāl*).[14] Al-Walīd also relates this tradition from his grandmother. Imām ad-Dāraquṭnī mentions that her state is also unknown.[15] In the opinion of the overwhelming majority of scholars, the existence of a narrator whose state is unknown would make the transmission conveyed by that chain weak.[16] This combination of two potentially weak narrators makes it questionable to use the tradition of Umm Waraqa as the basis for establishing any rulings in the Divine law. While the questionable nature of this tradition does not undermine the widespread acceptance it has received from the earlier scholars, it does make it difficult to use it as the primary evidence for a major precept of the religion, which is the case in this discussion. Were we to assume that the tradition is sound, it would still be difficult to use it as the basis for establishing the permissibility of a woman leading a public, mixed-gender obligatory congregational prayer, for reasons we shall now mention, if God so wills.

First of all, the Prophet ﷺ advised Umm Waraqa to stay in her house—*Qarri fī Baytiki*. This command is of import, as it creates two possible scenarios for the prayer she led. Either she remained in her house to lead the congregation, or she left her house to lead it in a mosque at an outside location. If she left her house to lead the prayer, she would have been acting contrary to the order of the Prophet ﷺ. There is no transmitted evidence that the prayer took place outside of her home. Hence, we can conclude that her mosque was in her house.

Her establishing the prayer in a mosque located in her home would be consistent with numerous narrations where the Prophet ﷺ permitted various companions to establish mosques in their homes.[17] Imām al-Bukhārī mentions that al-Barā' b. ᶜĀzib led congregational prayers in the mosque in his house (*Salla al-Barā' b. ᶜĀzib fī masjidihi fī dārihī jamāᶜatan*).[18] Imām al-Bukhārī also mentions a tradition where the Prophet ﷺ went to the house of a blind companion, 'Itbān b. Mālik, to establish a mosque there.[19] Ibn Mājah produces several narrations of this event.[20] In fact, the Prophet ﷺ ordered the generality of believers to establish mosques in their homes. ʿĀ'isha relates, "The Messenger of God ordered that mosques be established in the homes (*Dūr*, plural of *Dār*), and that they be cleaned and perfumed."[21]

Based on these and other relevant narrations, we can safely conclude that Umm Waraqa had a mosque in her house and that the prayer she led was not in a public place outside of her home. A more controversial point is who was being led in the prayer? Based on narrations describing Umm Waraqa's prayer there are three possibilities: her prayer caller (*muʿadhdhin*) and two servants, the women from the neighborhood surrounding her home, the women of her house. As for the first possibility, the wording of the tradition, along with the narrations we quoted above, would lead one to believe that the residents of her house were being led in the prayer. All of those narrations use *Dār* to refer to house. This would support the interpretation of *Dār* as "house" as opposed to "area." This interpretation is also consistent with the literal meaning of the term *Dār*. Al-Fayrūzabādī, Ibn Manẓūr, and Rāghib al-Iṣfahānī all define *Dār* as a walled structure encompassing a building and a courtyard.[22] An interpretative principle relates that "the origin in expressions is their literal meaning, there is no resorting to derived meanings without a decisive proof."[23] Hence, the term *Ahla Darīhā* would be best translated "the people of her house."

Based on what has been narrated, that would apparently include a male and female servant, along with the old man who was appointed by the Prophet ﷺ to serve as her prayer caller.[24] Reda rejects this interpretation, arguing that three people would not need a prayer caller.[25] This is not the case. Those scholars who consider the prayer call (*Adhān*) a right associated with the obligatory prayer or a right associated with the congregation hold it to be a highly desirable in deference to the prophetic practice (*Sunna*) to issue the call for any congregation assembled to undertake the five obligatory prayers.[26] The size of the congregation in this regard is irrelevant. According to a tradition mentioned by al-Bukhārī and others, even a person who is praying alone in an isolated area should make the call to prayer.[27] Hence, Reda's conclusion is not sound.

On the basis of this interpretation that the prayer was confined to the inhabitants of her house, it is related that Imāms al-Muzanī, aṭ-Ṭabarī, Abū Thawr, and Dāwūd aẓ-Ẓāhirī allowed for females to lead men in prayer.[28] Some modern scholars use this interpretation to allow for females to lead men in prayer in the confine of their homes, if the males lack the qualifications to lead the prayer.[29] The relevant point here is that the prayer was a private matter, conducted in the confines of Umm Waraqa's home, limited to the inhabitants of her house.

Were one to reject this first line of reasoning, a second possibility is that the people being led in prayer came from the area surrounding Umm Waraqa's home. This is the interpretation preferred by Reda. It has a basis in narrations from the Prophet ﷺ. In the tradition of 'Itbān b. Mālik, it is related that those referred to as "Ahli'd-Dār" used to gather there (*fathāba fī'l-bayt Rijālun min ahli'd-Dār*). Ibn Ḥajar mentions in his commentary on this tradition that *Ahli'd-Dār* refers to the people of the neighborhood (*al-Maḥallah*).[30]

Based on this understanding, it is not unreasonable to interpret *Ahla Dārihā,* in the tradition of Umm Waraqa, as the people of her "area," as Reda does. However, we are not left to guess as to who those people are. Imām ad-Dāraquṭnī's narration of this tradition mentions that Umm Waraqa was ordered to lead her women in prayer (*Nisā'ahā*).[31] Hence, if the people praying with Umm Waraqa were from the surrounding area, they were all women, as Imām ad-

Dāraquṭnī's version of the tradition makes clear. Here the text specifically states, "Her women." Ad-Dāraquṭnī's version would clarify a potentially vague expression in the other versions.

A third possibility, also based on joining between the majority narration and ad-Dāraquṭnī's version of the tradition, would lead us to understand that the people of Umm Waraqa's house were all women. Hence, the people of her house (*Ahla Dārihā*) being led in prayer were women. There is no transmitted evidence to the contrary, as the opinion that Ahla Dārihā were the two servants and the prayer caller, mentioned above, is an assumption. In *al-Mughnī*, Ibn Qudamā al-Maqdisī mentions the incumbency of accepting this third interpretation.[32] God knows best.

This latter understanding that Umm Waraqa only led women in prayer is strengthened by two ancillary evidences:

1. The numerous narrations mentioning that ʿĀ'isha, Umm Salama, and other female Companions led all women congregations.[33]
2. When the Prophet ﷺ established a mosque in the house of 'Itbān b. Mālik, the congregation was all male (*Rijulān min ahli'd-Dār*).

It would therefore make perfect sense for the Prophet to establish an all female congregation elsewhere.

Summary and Rulings

Based on the tradition of Umm Waraqa, its possible interpretations, and the other traditions mentioning women leading the prayer during the prophetic epoch, the Sunnī jurists have deduced the following rulings:

1. The Shāfiʿī and Ḥanbalī schools allow for a woman to lead other women in prayer without any restrictions. She can

lead such prayers in the mosque or other places. The Ḥanafīs permit a woman to lead other women in prayer. However, they hold it to be disliked.[34] All three of these schools stipulate that the woman leading the prayer should stand in the middle of the front row, without being in front of the women praying along with her. This is based on the description of the prayer led by ʿĀ'isha and Umm Salama. The Mālikīs hold that a woman cannot lead other women in the prayer.[35]

2. Of the three Sunnī schools that hold it permissible for a woman to lead other women in prayer, none of them hold it permissible for her to lead men in an obligatory prayer. There is a minority opinion in the Ḥanbalī school that permits a woman to lead men in Tarāwīḥ, a supererogatory prayer if certain conditions prevail, providing she stands behind them.[36]

3. Imām an-Nawawī mentions the following ruling in *al-Majmū'*, "If a woman leads a man or men in prayer, the prayer of the men is invalid. As for her prayer and the prayer of the women praying with her, it is sound."[37] As for the Friday prayer, he mentions that, "if a woman leads men in the Friday prayer, there are two rulings [concerning her prayer]. They have been mentioned by al-Qāḍī Abū Ṭayyib in his *Ta'līq*, the preponderant opinion is that her prayer is invalid, the second is that it is lawfully begun as the noon prayer."[38]

4. Some modern scholars hold it permissible for a woman to lead men in prayer within the confines of her house if there are no men qualified to lead the prayer.[39]

5. Imāms Abū Thawr, Dāwūd aẓ-Ẓāhirī, and aṭ-Ṭabarī, whose legal schools have been defunct for centuries, are related

to have held it permissible for a woman to lead men in prayer. This opinion is also related from Imām Muzanī, one of the principal narrators of the Shāfiʿī school. We will examine this issue in greater detail, as it serves as one of the evidences offered by Reda for the validity of unrestricted female prayer leadership.

The Rulings of al-Muzanī, Abū Thawr, Dāwūd aẓ-Ẓāhirī, and aṭ-Ṭabarī

As for the ancillary evidence ushered by Reda,[40] it is her saying:

> The above Prophetic tradition (*ḥadīth*) is the reason why several medieval Muslim scholars supported female leadership. These include Ṭabarī (d. 310 AH/923 CE), author of the famous Tafsīr: Jāmi' al-bayān wa ta'wīl āy al-Qur'ān and Tarīkh al-Rasūl wa'l Mulūk, Muzanī, Abū Thawr and Abū Sulaymān Dāwūd ibn Khalaf al-Iṣfahānī (d. 270 AH/884 CE), founder of the Zahirite school.[41]

We mention this evidence as ancillary because it cannot be the basis for establishing a ruling. None of the extant Sunnī schools consider the opinions of extinct schools as independently valid. This fact is not due to prejudice against the Imāms of the extinct schools and unjustly favoring those whose schools have survived. It is due to a simple methodological issue. Namely, neither the full corpus of rulings from the extinct schools, nor the details of their legal methodology have reached us in their entirety. Therefore, we do not know if a particular ruling attributed to an extinct school has been abrogated by another ruling in that school.

As for al-Muzanī, he was a qualified jurisconsult within the Shāfiʿī rite. However, it cannot be established with certainty that he founded an independent school.[42] It is known that he narrates, in his *Mukhtaṣir*, the accepted opinion of Imām ash-Shāfiʿī that a woman can only lead other women in the prayer.[43] It is also related in the *Mukhtaṣīr* that Imām al-Muzanī said:

> The prayer of anyone praying behind someone in a state of major ritual impurity, a woman, an insane person, or a disbeliever is acceptably conveyed if he is unaware of his/her (the Imām's) state.[44]

From this we can infer that the prayer of the follower in all of these scenarios is unacceptable if he knows of the Imām's state. This would include his prayer behind a woman. As for the opinion that Imām al-Muzanī actually endorsed female prayer leadership, it has not reached us in any extant document.

Concerning the opinion of Imām Dāwūd aẓ-Ẓāhirī, Ibn Ḥazm attempted to revive his school, based on a coherent, if debatable methodology.[45] This methodology led Ibn Ḥazm to some very liberal positions, such as an endorsement of music, and the permissibility of female prophets. However, on the issue of female prayer leadership, Ibn Ḥazm opined that it was forbidden by consensus. The point here is that, based based on Ibn Ḥazm's methodology, built on Imām Dāwūd's principles, an opinion contrary to that attributed to Imām Dāwūd on this issue has been reached.[46]

As for the reports of unrestricted female prayer leadership that are attributed to the Imāms we have mentioned, they have not reached us with unbroken chains, certainly not with irrefutable chains of transmission (*tawātur*), as is the case of the extant schools. In other words, there is no way for us to say with any degree of certainty that those opinions are indeed the opinions of Imāms aṭ-Ṭabarī, Abū Thawr, and Dāwūd aẓ-Ẓāhirī. That being the case, there is no basis to establish the preponderance of the position of the extinct schools over that of the extant schools.[47] Since the extant schools have a clear position on unrestricted female payer leadership and it is established at the highest level of proof, in the Sunnī rite,[48] a Sunnī is obliged to take that position. This obligation arises from a legislative principle, "Certainty cannot be cancelled by doubt."[49]

The Legislative Import of Prophetic Tradition (*Ḥadīth*)

The principal basis for Reda's argument for unrestricted prayer leadership is the tradition of Umm Waraqa. This position highlights her methodological inconsistency concerning prophetic tradition. In this instance, she accepts the Prophetic tradition. However, when the evidence advanced by tradition refutes her contentions, she discards the tradition in summary fashion. For example, she implies that the word for row (*ṣaff*) mentioned in a tradition narrated by Abū Hurayra has no connection to the prayers, rather it refers to "battle rows."[50] She arrives at this conclusion based on her position that this latter meaning of "row" is the only one that comes in the Qur'ān.

An objective examination of the relevant tradition reveals there is absolutely no way to support the conclusion that "row" has nothing to do with prayer. Examples of the use of the word row in connection to the prayer are too numerous to mention. For example, the Prophet ﷺ is related to have said just before the congregational prayer, "Straighten your rows (*ṣufuf*, plural of *ṣaff*), for straightening the rows is from the completion of the prayer (*Sawwu Ṣufūfakum fa inna Taswiya aṣ-Ṣaff min Tamām aṣ-Ṣalāt*)." Imām Muslim alone, in his rigorously authenticated collection of prophetic traditions, relates six versions of this instruction from four different Companions.[51] This tradition is also related by al-Bukhārī,[52] Abū Dāwūd,[53] at-Tirmidhī,[54] an-Nasāʿī,[55] and Ibn Mājah.[56]

She also mentions that there was no gender segregation in the Prophet's lifetime ﷺ, rather it was introduced later."[57] This claim is also refuted by prophetic tradition. In addition to the tradition narrated by Abū Hurayrah,[58] which Reda dismisses, there is overwhelming evidence to support gender segregation during worship services.

As for gender segregation in the prayer, again, proof for that during the prophetic epoch is irrefutable. I will relate a few instructive examples. Imām al-Bukhārī relates in his rigorously authenticated collection of tradition, from Anas b. Mālik, "I prayed along with an orphan boy behind the Prophet ﷺ in my house. My mother, Umm Sulaym, [prayed] behind us."[59] There are numerous other sound narrations of this tradition.

Another tradition relates that there was an extremely beautiful woman who used to pray in the congregation behind the Prophet ﷺ. Some of the men would hasten to the front row of men in order not to be distracted by her. Others would procrastinate in order to be in the last row of men to look behind themselves at her when they bowed during the prayer.[60] This arrangement of the men in front of the women in the congregational prayer led by the Prophet ﷺ is affirmed by the Qur'ān, as this incident was the occasion for the revelation of the verse, *We know those of you who hasten forward [to the front prayer rows], and we know those who lag behind.* [15:24][61]

Imāms al-Bukhārī[62] and Muslim[63] mention a tradition relating that the Prophet ﷺ used to address the women separately on the day of *ʿĪd*. One of Imām al-Bukhārī's versions is particularly instructive as it mentions, "...then he [the Prophet] advanced, splitting them [the rows of men] until he came to the women."[64] He would then address them and exhort them to give charity. The point here is that if the men and women were not segregated, as is the custom in our congregational prayers until today, why would the Prophet ﷺ have to wade through the men to reach the women? He would have had to first gather the women. Hence, any claim that there was no gender segregation during the prophetic epoch is baseless. We could bring many more examples to prove this point, but what we have mentioned should suffice.

Similarly, Reda avoids the implications of tradition when she states, "Moreover, of the numerous occurrences in the Qur'ān of fitna or its derivatives, none apply to women."[65] Based on this and the authority of G.H.A. Juynboll, she concludes "...a ḥadīth in which the Prophet supposedly referred to women as constituting man's greatest fitna in life"[66] is "unreliable."

As for the ḥadīth in question, it reads, "I have not left a tribulation (*fitna*) more harmful to men than women." Al-Bukhārī,[67] Muslim,[68] and at-Tirmidhī[69] have all related this tradition. Although we could discuss its meaning, the report itself is rigorously authenticated. As for the authority of Juynboll, Harald Motzki has demonstrated the unreliable nature of Juynboll's ḥadīth scholarship. In discussing Juynboll's effort to discredit all of the narrations from Nāfi' on the authority of Ibn ʿUmar, Motzki shows that his premises, conclusions, and methodology are all flawed. He notes:

> The point of departure for our investigation has been the hypothesis that the main conclusions of Juynboll's study on Nāfi' are not tenable. One of his hypotheses claimed that all of the Prophetical ahadīth with the isnad Nāfi'—ibn ʿUmar found in the "canonical" collections, which are highly esteemed amongst Muslims—do not go back to Nāfi' but rather to Mālik b. Anas.[70] We were able to show, using the same examples as Juynboll, namely the ḥadīth on the alms of the breaking of the fast, that his hypothesis is wrong. There is no doubt that this ḥadīth goes back to Ibn ʿUmar and was not invented by Mālik.[71]

Motzki further states:

> Juynboll's conclusions in his article on Nāfi' are generalizations. They are not limited to the analyzed example, the zakat al-fitr ḥadīth, but are judgments on all the Nāfi'—Ibn ʿUmar—ahadīth. Since we were able to prove Juynboll's conclusions wrong in at least one case, his general statements can be refuted.[72]

Reda presents the thinking of the orthodoxy on the issue of scholarly consensus (*Ijmā'*) as a state of confusion. This disguises the fact that after the initial centuries of debate, most of the Sunnī scholars were able to settle on a consistent definition of scholarly consensus. Wahba az-Zuḥaylī captures this meaning with the following definition, "The agreement of the qualified scholars from the Community of Muḥammad ﷺ on a legislative ruling, after his death, during any subsequent era."[73] As this definition hinges on the agreement of qualified scholars in a particular era, the consensus claimed by Ibn Ḥazm concerning unrestricted female payer leadership would not be impossible. The Kharijites, due to their literalism, are not known to have produced high-level scholars. Hence, in the era that consensus may have occurred on the issue of unrestricted female payer leadership, there could well have been no qualified scholars among the Kharijites to dissent. As for groups such as the Ja'farī Shiites and the Zaydis, who generally have a different understanding of the legislative import of consensus, their ruling on the issue being discussed agrees with the position of the Sunnīs. Hence, there would likely be no dissension from their camp. As for the opinions of al-Muzanī, Abū Thawr, Dāwūd aẓ-Ẓāhirī, and aṭ-Ṭabarī, we have mentioned some considerations earlier that would lead us to reject any statement attributed to them on this issue as being definitive. Surely, God knows best.

Conclusion

The other evidences mentioned by Reda, numbered from 3-7, dealing with the Qur'ānic story of the Queen of Sheba, gender justice, gender discrimination, justice in general, and the need for men to listen to women, will not be dealt with in this article because they have no bearing on the derivation of legal rulings.[74] However, they are of importance in determining how existing rulings are to be understood and implemented. In this regard, Reda's appeal for greater compassion, justice, and understanding is appreciated.

From what we have presented above, it should be clear that a woman leading a mixed gender, public, obligatory congregational prayer is not something sanctioned by Islamic law in the Sunnī tradition. Her leading the Friday congregational prayer is even more unfounded, as she would be required to do things that are forbidden or disliked for her in other prayers. Saying this, we should not lose sight of the fact that there are many issues in our community involving the neglect, oppression, and in some instances, the degradation of our women. Until we address those issues as a community, in an enlightened manner, we are open to criticism and will likely encourage various forms of protest.

In addition to gender issues, we are faced by many other nagging concerns. These problems defy simplistic solutions. Only through the attainment of the prophetic virtues that Islam seeks to cultivate in it adherents will we have a chance to even begin dealing with them. One of the greatest of these virtues is humility. Perhaps, if the men of our community had more humility, we would behave in ways that do not alienate, frustrate, or outright oppress our women. Greater humility will help immensely in improving our condition. Our Prophet ﷺ has said in that regard, "No one humbles himself/herself for the sake of God except God elevates him/her."[75] In addition to this elevation, another interpretation of this tradition is that the esteem of the humble person will be magnified in the hearts of others. Certainly, a healthier appreciation of each other would go a long way towards relieving the growing tension between the sexes in some quarters of our community.

We must also understand that Islam has never advocated a strict liberationist philosophy.[76] Our fulfillment in this life will never come as the result of breaking real or perceived chains of oppression. That does not mean that we should not struggle against oppressive practices and institutions. Islam enjoins us to do so. However, when we understand that success in such worldly struggles has nothing to do with our fulfillment as human beings, we will be able to keep those struggles in perspective and not be moved to frustration or despair when their outcomes are counter to our plans.

Our fulfillment does not lie in our liberation, rather it lies in the conquest of our soul and its base desires. That conquest only occurs through our enslavement to God. Our enslavement to God in turn means that we have to suppress many of our souls' desires and inclinations. Therein is one of the greatest secrets to unleashing our real human potential. This is so because it is our spiritual potential that separates us from the rest of this creation, and it is to the extent that we are able to conquer our physical nature that we realize that spiritual potential.

We must all realize that we will never achieve any meaningful change in our situation relying on our own meager resources. The great sage Ibn ʿAṭā Allāh as-Sakandarī has said, "Nothing you seek through your Lord will ever be difficult; and nothing you seek through yourself will ever be easy."[77] Now is the time to give ourselves wholeheartedly to our Lord. The trials and tribulations we are currently witnessing will only intensify as we move closer to the end of time. If we are not living for our Lord, relying on His guidance and help, and trusting in His wisdom, we will find it very difficult to negotiate our way through this world.

When we live for our Lord it becomes easy to live with each other. If in our personal relations we can come to embody the spirit of mutual love, mercy, and affection, encouraged by our Prophet ﷺ, we will be able to live together in harmony and make a beautiful and lasting contribution towards the uplift of men and women alike. The times we live in cry out for such a contribution. The question is, "Who will respond?"

Notes

1 Quoted in Ibn Ḥumayd, *Naḍra an-Naʿīm*, 5180.

2 Ibn Ḥumayd, *Naḍra an-Naʿīm*, 5178.

3 See Nevin Reda, *What Would the Prophet Do? The Islamic Basis for Female-Led Prayer*, March 10, 2005, at <http://www.muslimwakeup.com/main/archives/2005/03/002706print.php>.

4 Reda, 1.

5 Imām Muḥammad al-ʿAẓīmabādī, *ʿAwn al-Ma'būd Sharḥ Sunan Abū Dāwūd* (Beirut: Dār al-Kitāb al-ʿArabī, nd), 2:300-301, no. 577-578.

6 Imām ʿAli b. ʿUmar ad-Dāraquṭnī, *Sunan ad-Dāraquṭnī* (Beirut: Dār al-Kutub al-ʿIlmiyya, 1417 AH/1996 CE), 1:284, no. 1071.

7 Al-Bayhaqī, 3:186-187.

8 Imām Muḥammad b. ʿAbdullāh al-Ḥākim, *al-Mustadrak ʿalā aṣ-Ṣaḥīḥayn* (Beirut: Dār al-Kutub al-ʿIlmiyya, 1411 AH/1990 CE), 1:320, no. 730.

9 Muḥammad b. Sa'd az-Zuhrī, *aṭ-Ṭabaqāt al-Kubrā* (Beirut: Dār Iḥyā' at-Tarāth al-ʿArabī), 8:460, no. 4610.

10 See Aḥmad Khan, trans., *Sunan Abū Dāwūd* (Lahore: Sh. Muḥammad Ashraf, 1984), 1:155-156.

11 His name is properly pronounced in the diminutive form Jumay' as opposed to Jāmi'. See Ibn Ḥajar al-ʿAsqalānī, *Tahẓīb at-Tahẓīb* (Beirut: Dār al-Ma'rifa, 1417 AH/1996 CE), 6:87.

12 See Shams ad-Din Muḥammad b. Aḥmad adh-Dhahabī, *Mīzān al-'Itidāl* (Beirut: Dār al-Kutub al-ʿIlmiyya, 1416 AH/1995 CE), 7:129.

13 Ibn Ḥajar al-ʿAsqalānī, *at-Tahẓīb*, 6:88.

14 See Ibn Ḥajar al-ʿAsqalānī, *Taqrīb at-Tahẓīb* (Beirut: Mu'assah ar-Risāla, 1420 AH/1999 CE), 281; Ibn Ḥajar, *at-Tahẓīb*, 3:339.

15 Ad-Dāraquṭnī, 1: 284, no. 1071. Imām ad-Dāraquṭnī mentions al-Walīd as narrating the tradition from "his mother."

16 See Imām Jalāl'ad-dīn as-Suyūṭī, *Tadrīb ar-Rāwī* (Beirut: Dār al-Kitāb al-ʿArabī, 1417 AH/1996 CE), 1:268; Mullā ʿAli al-Qāri', *Sharḥ Nukhba al-Fikr* (Beirut: Dār al-Arqam, nd), 519.

17 Imām al-Bukhārī has included a section in his compendium of rigorously authenticated ahadīth entitled, "Mosques in the Houses." See Ibn Ḥajar al-ʿAsqalānī, *Fatḥ al-Bārī,* 1:672.

18 Ibn Ḥajar al-ʿAsqalānī, section 46.

19 Ibn Ḥajar al-ʿAsqalānī, no. 425.

20 Ibn Mājah, 108, no. 755.

21 Ibn Mājah, 108, no. 759.

22 Ṭāḥir Aḥmad Zāwī, *Tartib al-Qāmūs al-Muḥīt* (Beirut: Dār al-Fikr, nd), 2:229; Ibn Manẓūr, 5:325; Al-Isfahānī, 321.

23 An-Nadwī, 223.

24 See al-ʿAẓīmabādī, 301-303.

25 Reda, 4.

26 For the Shāfiʿī position on this issue see ash-Shirbīnī, *Mughnī al-Muḥtāj* 1:209.

27 Ibn Ḥajar al-ʿAsqalānī, *Fatḥ al-Bārī*, 2:116, no. 609;

28 We will discuss the opinions of these four Imāms subsequently.

29 ʿAbd al-Karīm az-Zaydān, *al-Mufaṣṣal fī Aḥkām al-Marʿa wa'l Bayt al-Muslim* (Beirut: Mu'assa ar-Risāla, 1410 AH/1994 CE), 1:252. Muḥammad b. Ismaʿil aṣ-Ṣanāʿī, *Subul as-Salām* (Beirut: Dār al-Kutub al-ʿIlmiyya), 2:76.

30 Ibn Ḥajar al-ʿAsqalānī, *Fatḥ al-Bārī*, 1:675.

31 Ad-Dāraquṭnī, *aṣ-Ṣunan*, 1:284, no. 1071.

32 See Muwaffaq ad-Dīn b. Qudama al-Maqdisī, *al-Mughnī* (Beirut: Dār al-Fikr, nd), 2:34.

33 For examples of these narrations see al-ʿAẓīmabādī, 2:301-302; al-Bayhaqī, 3:186-187; Muḥammad b. Idrīs ash-Shāfiʿī, *Kitāb al-Umm* (Beirut: Dār al-Fikr, 1403 AH/1983 CE), 8:117. Az-Zaydān, 1:251-256.

34 See Muḥammad Amīn b. ʿAbidīn, *Hāshiya Radd al-Mukhtār* (Beirut: Dār al-Fikr, 1415 AH/1995 CE), 1:609; ʿAlāʿad-Dīn b. Masʿūd al-Kasānī, *Badāʿī aṣ-Ṣanāʿī fī Tartīb ash-Sharāʿi* (Beirut: Dār al-Kutub al-ʿIlmiyya, 1407 AH/1986 CE), 1:157.

35 See Aḥmad Zarrūq and Qāsim b. ʿIsā at-Tannūkhī, *Sharḥ ʿAlā Matn ar-Risālah* (Beirut: Dār al-Fikr, 1402 AH/1986 CE), 1:192.

36 For the Ḥanafī position on this issue see Ibn ʿĀbidīn, 1:609; for the Shāfiʿī position see an-Nawawī, *Kitāb al-Majmū'*, 4:151-152. For the Ḥanbalī position see, Ibn Qudāma, *al-Mughnī*, 2:34.

37 An-Nawawī, *al-Majmū'*, 4:152.

38 An-Nawawī, *al-Majmū'*, 4:165.

39 See aṣ-Ṣanāʿī, *Subul as-Salām*, 2:76; az-Zaydān, *al-Mufaṣṣal*, 1:252.

40 I use the term "ancillary" to describe this "evidence" as it cannot serve as a primary source of legal rulings. In some circumstances, it could possibly support or strengthen a ruling established by one of the primary sources of law. Hence, its description as ancillary.

41 Reda, 1-2.

42 Muḥammad Hāshim Kamālī, *Principles of Islamic Jurisprudence* (Cambridge: Islamic Texts Society, 2003), 491-492.

43 See ash-Shāfiʿī, *Kitāb al-Umm*, 8:117.

44 Ash-Shāfiʿī, 116.

45 See Ibn Ḥazm al-Andalusī, *Al-Iḥkām fī Uṣūl al-Aḥkām*, Aḥmad Shākir, ed., (Beirut: Dār al-Āfāq al-Jadīda, 1980). The differences between the methodology of Ibn Ḥazm and the mainstream Sunnīs have been most prominently highlighted by Imām al-Bājī. See, Al-Muṣṭafā al-Wadīfī, *al-Munāẓara fī Uṣūl ash-Sharīʿah al-Islamīyya: Dirāsa fī at-Tanāẓur bayna Ibn Ḥazm wa'l-Bājī*, (Ribāṭ: Ministry of Endowments and Religious Affairs, Kingdom of Morocco, 1419 AH/1998 CE).

46 Ibn Ḥazm, *Marātib al-'Ijmā'* (Beirut: Dār Ibn Ḥazm, 1419 AH/1998 CE), 51.

47 This point is made for the sake of argument. In reality, the issue under discussion is not one that is eligible to be settled by establishing preponderance, because one of the conditions for such issues is that the two opposing positions be acceptable for establishing a ruling. See Imām Sayfuddīn b. Ābī ʿAli al-Āmidī, *Al-Iḥkām fī Uṣūl al-Aḥkām* (Beirut: Dār al-Kutub al-ʿIlmiyya, 1405 AH/1985 CE), 4:460.

48 The prohibition of unrestricted female payer leadership is established by the consensus of the four Sunnī Imāms: Abū Ḥanīfa, Mālik, ash-Shāfiʿī, and Aḥmad. A generally accepted principle among the Sunnīs is that what the four Imāms agree on is a binding ruling. In the last section of his treatise on the Creed of the Sunnīs, Muwaffaq b. Qudāma al-Maqdisī writes, "Association with one of the Imāms in jurisprudential matters, such as the four Sunnī schools, is not condemnable. Their (the Imāms) differing in legal rulings is a mercy. Those who differed among them are praised for their differences, rewarded for their assertion [in trying to ascertain the truth]. [Again,] their differing is an expansive mercy, and what they agreed on is a decisive proof." Muwaffaq b. Qudamāh al-Maqdisī, *al-'Itiqād* (Cairo: Maktaba al-Qur'ān, nd), 75. Ibn Ḥazm, and others claim that the prohibition of unrestricted female prayer leadership is established by binding consensus. See Imām Ibn Ḥazm, *Marātib*, 51. Were it indeed the case that binding consensus has occurred on this issue, to reject it would be considered extremely grave in the Sunnī tradition.

49 An-Nadwī, *al-Qawāʿid*, 105.

50 Reda, 7.

51 An-Nawawī, *al-Minhāj*, 4:376-388, nos. 974-979.

52 Ibn Ḥajar al-ʿAsqalānī, *Fatḥ al-Bārī*, 2:272, no. 723.

53 Abū Dāwūd, 107, no. 668.

54 At-Tirmidhī, 72, no. 227.

55 An-Nasāʾī, 112, nos. 812-814.

56 Ibn Mājah, 140, nos. 993-994.

57 Reda, 7.

58 Reda, 7.

59 Ibn Ḥajar al-ʿAsqalānī, *Fatḥ al-Bārī*, 275, no. 727.

60 This narration is produced by Imām al-Bayhaqī in his collection. Al-Bayhaqī, 3:139, nos. 5169, and 5170.

61 Al-Qur'ān 15:24. For an explanation of the circumstance surrounding the revelation of this verse see Imām Jalāl'ad-dīn as-Suyūṭī, *Lubāb an-Nūqul fī Asbāb an-Nuzūl* (Beirut: Dār al-Ma'rifa, 1418 AH/1997 CE), 172. This tradition is also related by at-Tirmidhī, an-Nasāʾī, al-Ḥākim, and others.

62 Ibn Ḥajar al-ʿAsqalānī, *Fatḥ al-Bārī*, 2:601, no. 978-979.

63 An-Nawawī, *al-Minhāj*, 3:420-421, no. 2054.

64 Ibn Ḥajar al-ʿAsqalānī, *Fatḥ al-Bārī*, 2:601, no. 978-979.

65 Reda, 8.

66 Reda, 8.

67 Ibn Ḥajar al-ʿAsqalānī, *Fatḥ al-Bārī*, 9:172, no. 5096.

68 An-Nawawī, *al-Minhāj*, 9:57, no. 6880.

69 At-Tirmidhī, 627-628, no. 2780.

70 Juynboll alleges that Imām Mālik fabricated all of the *ahadīth* he relates from Nāfi'.

71 Harald Motzki, "Whither ḥadīth-studies? A Critical examination of G.H.A. Juynboll's Nāfi' the mawla of Ibn ʿUmar, and his position in Muslim *Ḥadīth*–Literature Part 2" trans. Frank Griffel. *Der Islam* 73 (1996): 1.

72 Motzki, 18.

73 Wahba az-Zuḥaylī, *Uṣūl al-Fiqh al-Islāmī*, (Beirut: Dār al-Fikr, 1418 AH/1998 CE) 1:490.

74 Reda, 2.

75 An-Nawawī, *al-Minhāj*, 9:358, no. 6535.

76 By strict liberationist philosophy, I refer to the idea that the elimination of real or imagined forms of oppression will result in the end of human alienation, lack of fulfillment, or other negative psychologi-

cal states. An illustration of a liberationist philosophy, consistent with this meaning, is Marxism, which posits that once the oppression of capitalism is eradicated human alienation will end as humans appropriate their formerly usurped production.

77 ʿAbdul-Majīd ash-Sharnūbī, *Sharḥ al-Ḥikam al-ʿAṭāʿiyya* (Damascus: Dār Ibn Kathīr, 1413 AH/1992 CE), 38.

Made in the USA